Praise for Peter Cashorali's *Fairy Tales*

"In addition to being wonderfully entertaining, Cashorali's yarns are also poignant morality tales. . . . From the first page to the last, the reader is taken along with the characters on a somewhat mystical journey. With Cashorali's pervasive wit and keen flair for anachronistic irony, half the fun is getting there."

—*Washington Blade*

"Enchanting . . . the sort of romantic bedtime storytelling which can help out marriages. Try it."

—*Frontiers*

"With their tender, queer twist, Peter Cashorali's smart, saucy retelling of the classics will nurture the child giving life to every gay man—and give us myths to live and laugh by."

—Richard Labonte, general manager, A Different Light Bookstores

"Lovely, mesmerizing, and often deeply moving; tales of contemporary lovers told with the rhythmic cadences, moral urgency, and shimmering supernaturalism of classic folk tales. Read and—even better—reread them."

—Robert Rodi, author of *Fag Hag, Closet Case*, and *What They Did to Princess Paragon*

"Cashorali's enchanting stories are as wise as they are witty . . . taking us down roads we scarcely dared to dream about as children. The Brothers Grimm go gay in all best senses of the word."

—Mark Thompson, author of *Gay Soul*

"Sexy, radical poetic, and acutely human, Cashorali's fantastic bundle of fairy tales helps restore to gay men the patrimony, the psychic maps, and the Eros that have been stolen from us. The contemporary, erotic edge to his work shows that we queers are living a new myth, weirdly futuristic and archaic at the same time."

—Douglas Sadownick, author of *Sacred Lips of the Bronx* and *Sex Between Men*

"Peter Cashorali's *Fairy Tales* are told with an enduring wit and wisdom. The images, both comic and haunting, have resonated long after my lover and I read them to each other. This is an enchanting—even poetic—book that is a welcome and necessary addition to gay culture."

—Kenny Fries, author of *The Healing Notebooks* and *Body, Remember*

"Ogres, frogs, and a cat the color of something difficult to see: [*Fairy Tales* is] a book whose pages are mirrors of our lives, inner and outer, real and imagined."

—Andrew Ramer, author of *Ask Your Angels* and *Revelations for a New Millennium*

FAIRY TALES

TRADITIONAL STORIES
RETOLD FOR GAY MEN

Peter Cashorali

Foreword by Robert H. Hopcke

HarperSanFrancisco
An Imprint of HarperCollinsPublishers

For Caesar Alberto Bonilla,

the man who was lovers with a pigeon,

this book and its author.

HarperSanFrancisco and the author, in association with The Basic Foundation, a not-for-profit organization whose primary mission is reforestation, will facilitate the planting of two trees for every one tree used in the manufacture of this book.

A TREE CLAUSE BOOK

"The Golden Key" was previously published in *Queer Spirits: A Gay Men's Myth Book*, ed. Will Roscoe (Boston: Beacon Press, 1995).

HarperCollins Web Site: http://www.harpercollins.com

HarperCollins®, ◼®, and HarperSanFrancisco™ are trademarks of HarperCollins Publishers Inc.

Illustrations by Brian Williams

FIRST HARPERCOLLINS PAPERBACK EDITION PUBLISHED IN 1997

Library of Congress Cataloging-in-Publication Data
Cashorali, Peter.
Fairy tales : traditional tales retold for gay men / Peter Cashorali ; foreword by Robert H. Hopcke. — 1st ed.
ISBN 0-06-251308-7 (cloth)
ISBN 0-06-251309-5 (pbk.)
1. Gay men—Fiction. 2. Fairy tales—Adaptations.
I. Title
PS3553.A79393F35   1995   95-14185
813'.54—dc20

03 04 05 ❖ HAD 10 9

TABLE OF CONTENTS

Source Abbreviations

A   *The Apocrypha*, Edgar J. Goodspeed, translator
AFT   *Arab Folktales*, Inea Bushnaq, editor
AL   *The Andrew Lang Fairy Tale Treasury*, Andrew Lang
B   *Bajka*, Aleksander Puszkin (translated for the present author by Andrzej Wilczak)
BBFF   *The Borzoi Book of French Folktales*, Paul Delarue, editor
BLF   *Best-Loved Folktales of the World*, Joanna Cole, editor
EV   *Elijah's Violin*, Howard Schwartz
GB   *The Complete Fairy Tales of the Brothers Grimm*, Jack Zipes, translator
GDF   *Grateful Dead Folktales*, Bob Franzosa, editor
GFT   *Gypsy Folktales*, Diane Tong, editor
HCA   *The Complete Hans Christian Andersen Fairy Tales*, Lily Owens, editor
IF   *Italian Folktales*, Italo Calvino
IndF   *Individuation in Fairy Tales*, Marie-Louise von Franz
NFT   *Norwegian Folktales*, Peter Christian Asbjornsen and Jorgen Moe
PCFT   *Perrault's Complete Fairy Tales*, Charles Perrault and Mme. Leprince de Beaumont
RFT   *Russian Fairy Tales*, Aleksandr Afana'sev, editor
SFFT   *Scandinavian Folk and Fairy Tales*, Claire Booss, editor

FOREWORD

Telling a story is a sacred act of creation. In the stories of a people one can find the accumulated wisdom of hundreds, sometimes thousands of years of shared experience, the inherent conflicts and values of an entire culture, an understanding of what it means to be human and what place we occupy in the universe. When I tell you a story, I bring you closer to me in an act of love, sharing with you what I hold most dear, and guiding you along with what knowledge I have gleaned through the exhilarating, agonizing, and confusing journey of life. Generations of women have told stories to their daughters and to each other to remind themselves who they are, what they care about, and how to proceed wisely, just as men, since the beginning of language itself, have told their sons and each other stories of how the world came to be and why men are men. The act of storytelling expresses the character of a people while at the same time creating the very community that has given rise to the story. Telling a story is a sacred act of creation.

Storytelling is an art, and among all the arts, the art of the folktale holds a special place for those of us who love language, because a folktale, as many a writer, psychologist, anthropologist, and linguist has discovered, is unlike any other narrative. Its characters are at once particular individuals and universal types. Its plots are filled with unique and amazing occurrences that have the feeling of everyday events in response to which we can all say, "Yes, that happened to me, too." Listening to a folktale's repetitions and meanderings we feel both familiar and strange, comforted and challenged, betwixt and between. Whereas fiction, as the term is commonly understood, attempts to tell one person's story, and thereby touch a universal chord, while the holy writ of a culture attempts to tell a universal story and thereby touch the individual, the folktale stands in the middle and does both at once. For this reason, the artist who can capture the stories of a culture, who can tell a folktale and do it justice, is an artist indeed.

Telling a folktale is a natural art, but writing a folktale down is an act of translation. As the interest in folktales grew in Europe and as writers created literary collections of their own country's folktales, the true art of spoken narrative became like a butterfly pinned upon the page, preserved under glass. What once was free, ephemeral, and alive was now caught, beautiful but unmoving. It required, therefore, an even greater artist to make this rendering live once more, to make this translation from the living voice into a true tale that you could not only hear in your head as you read it but also continue to hear in your ears. Charles Perrault, the Brothers Grimm, Hans Christian Anderson, Italo Calvino—these translators succeeded, and their fame is deserved.

With this volume of *Fairy Tales*, Peter Cashorali follows in a long line of storytellers before him. In the sacred act of telling these stories over the years before this book was written, he stood before many people and viva voce spoke the truth of his community, my community, by telling the stories that follow. The rich wisdom of these tales is a wisdom that gay men need to hear, and the lessons that the men in these stories learn through their encounters with glamorous witches, sadistic ogres, clever animals, wicked brothers, and enchanted objects are lessons that bear repeating to everyone, but especially to men in the gay community.

Trust yourself. Do not base your life on superficiality. Help others when you can. Do not resist your destiny. Everyone ages. You cannot escape death. Above all, love. Love, and love as your heart directs you, for to love truly and deeply is never wrong.

With great skill, Peter has created a collection of folktales that, as all such tales do, point simultaneously to the particular and the universal, and he has done so, as all literary collections of such tales must, through translation. Thus, the men who love men in these stories are who they are: Robert and his wise grandmother; Romaine and his bittersweet love for the lost soul Sean; Jeffrey and his magic dog, Penny Loafers. Each one embodies the Everyman of every folktale—he who is turned out of his home by selfish relatives and must find his own way forward back home, he who searches for the perfect partner in a quest filled with adventures and heartbreak, he who one day by accident comes across someone or something that transforms his life forever. In a brilliant act of translation, Peter has carried these timeless tales into the contemporary gay milieu—into our own mythic land of boutiques and coffee shops, penniless youths and rich A-gays, hairdressers and personal trainers, dinner parties and decorated condos, sugar daddies and trolls, bestial tops and subservient bottoms—and in doing so, he has made these familiar tales amazingly and unavoidably personal. What gay man will read "The Ugly Duckling" and not feel the pain of growing up different? Who can, since AIDS, read "Godfather Death" and not feel that wish we have so often felt to cheat death, just this once, and hold on to someone we love? How many gay men reading "The Man Who Was Lovers with a Pigeon" can honestly say they never secretly wished for others to envy them for their beautiful lovers?

An adventure awaits you, reader, in the stories to come, the stories of your life and mine. Tarry with me no longer, for I am just the lowly introducer, and make your way onward. One word of advice, though, first, humbly offered to you and sincerely. Read what follows not with your eyes, but with your heart, as these are, above all, stories of the heart, and in reading, may you find yours—and your fairy tale—within! Now, that's enough. On you go . . .

Robert H. Hopcke

THE GOLDEN KEY

ONCE, ON THE other side of the mountains, on the edge of the Endless Forest, a boy lived in a cottage with his mother and father, his brothers and sisters. It was winter, the coldest winter the boy had ever experienced, the coldest winter anyone could remember in a land memorable for the coldness of its winters, and there was no firewood in the cottage for the boy. There was firewood for his brothers, who would grow up to be just like their father, and firewood for his sisters, who would grow up to be just like their mother. But for the boy, who would grow up to be like himself and no other, there was none.

One morning the boy woke up before sunrise. The night had been the coldest one yet, and the frost lay heavy on his blankets. The boy determined that rather than spend another such night, he'd go into the forest and get firewood for himself. He dressed and left the cottage while everyone slept, dragging his sled behind him over the snowy fields and under the eaves of the forest. Here everything was frozen and silent, and because the winter had been so hard there wasn't much wood to be found. The boy ventured deeper into the forest, finding a few twigs here, a pinecone there, a fallen branch further on, and gradually he loaded his sled.

"The Golden Key," GB.

By the time he had enough wood, he was so cold and had wandered so far that he decided to build a fire for himself right where he was. He was brushing the snow away when suddenly the sun, which had risen while he searched, gleamed on something at his feet. The boy saw it was a key, a golden key, and he picked it up eagerly. "It's mine," he laughed, tossing it into the air and catching it, and the key sparkled and glittered in the sunlight as if it were laughing with him.

After a while it occurred to him that where there was a key, there must be a lock that opened to it. He swept the snow away all around him; then, finding nothing, he began digging into the ground. Oh, the ground was hard, harder than stone, harder than steel, and the boy had no tools to work with but his hands. It was a long while that he dug, but whenever he got tired or discouraged he pulled the golden key out of his pocket and let his eyes rest on its promise, and then went back to his labor refreshed.

At last he uncovered a small iron chest and pried it away from the grip of the frozen earth. He turned it in his hands, searching for a lock, and at first it seemed there was none. The boy was patient, though, and at last he found one, so small he'd missed it before. He fit the key into the lock and began to turn it. And now we must wait for him to unlock his chest completely and lift its lid, before we learn what its wonderful contents are and how they change his life in ways no one could have imagined.

THE VAMPIRE

O NCE, IN A small city not far from here, there was a tradition that the young men and women celebrated the Easter season with six nights of parties. The nights were just starting to grow warmer, and it was that time in their lives when the young people were free from the restrictions of being children and not yet under the restrictions of marrying and having children of their own. It was a brief time, and they were encouraged to enjoy it while it lasted.

A young man was at such a party. There were good things to eat, and music, and young women to talk and laugh and flirt with, but the young man was restless and dissatisfied. Outside, the ground was loosening itself for spring, and the young man, whose name was Robert, felt that he also was loosening, getting ready, but he didn't know for what.

A man arrived at the party whom no one could remember seeing before. He was handsome, his eyes were bright, his clothes were the latest fashion. Soon it became apparent that the handsome stranger knew just what to say to charm everyone. He danced with all the young women until they wanted to dance with no one else. And he had a laugh that made everyone who heard it want to laugh as well. He talked, he danced, he was at everyone's side, but all night he kept his eye on Robert.

"A Lost Shoe of Gold," AFT; "The Virgin Mary's Child," GB; "The Vampire," RFT.

At midnight the handsome stranger said it was time for him to leave. Everyone protested and said the evening was just beginning, but the stranger wouldn't be persuaded to stay longer. He turned to Robert. "Perhaps Robert will walk me out to the street," he said.

Robert was suddenly shy, but his best friend took him aside. "What's the matter?" the friend asked. "He's a fine person. Walk him out to the street." And so Robert agreed to do so.

They stood under the night sky and talked a while, the stranger just outside the gate, Robert just inside. "You'd like my home," the stranger said.

"Where are you from?" Robert asked, though he felt the stranger was right.

The stranger looked back toward the house where the young men and the young women were dancing together. "I'm not from here," he said.

Just then a cloud passed over the face of the moon, and when it had gone so had the stranger. Robert stepped out into the street, but in both directions as far as he could see it was empty.

Next night there was a second party at another house. The young women were laughing, the young men boasting, but to Robert it seemed dull, and he wondered if anyone had thought to give the handsome stranger the address. And then the stranger arrived. He danced with the young women, he laughed with the young men, but all evening long he kept his eye on Robert.

When midnight came he asked Robert to walk out with him and Robert went gladly. They stood a while and talked, the stranger just outside the gate, Robert just inside. The music from indoors sounded small in the night air, and the stranger said, "There are other places to be."

And Robert, who had always hoped there were, said, "Where?"

"You'll like it there," the stranger promised.

Just then a moth darted at Robert's face and made him blink, and when he looked the stranger was gone. He ran to the corner and looked up and down the boulevard, but there was no one there.

Robert wanted to find out where the stranger went. He wondered if his parents might know how to do this, but recently he'd noticed that whenever there was a mystery, they seemed as mystified as anyone. Then he thought of his very old grandmother, and he determined to ask her.

The next day he traveled across the city to the apartment where his grandmother lived. She was in her parlor, surrounded by statues of the saints and candles burning in red glasses. He sat on her sofa and said, "Nana, how can I find out where someone goes who disappears too fast for me to see?"

"Why should you know?" she asked.

But he was insistent. "Please, Nana," he said. "I have to know where he goes."

She took a spool of thread out of her sewing basket. "Take this and make a loop in one end of the thread," she told him. "Slip the loop over a button on this person's clothes and let the spool unwind. Follow the thread."

Robert thanked his grandmother and left. That night he brought the spool of thread to the party. There was music, and laughter, and in the corners young men and women made secret plans to marry in the summer. Robert waited. Finally the handsome stranger arrived, and he was whisked into the center of the room where he told stories until everyone else forgot to talk. But all evening he kept his eye on Robert, and Robert kept his eye on him.

When it was time for the stranger to leave, Robert was right beside him. "Let me walk you to the street," he said, and the stranger smiled at him. They left the party and stood a while, talking, the stranger just outside the gate, Robert just inside.

"Soon," the stranger said.

And Robert, who could feel this was so, said, "But when?"

"Why, we're almost there now," the stranger smiled, and Robert slipped the looped thread over a button on his shirt. Just then the breeze

blew a bit of dust into his eye, and when he blinked it away the stranger
had gone. But the spool of thread danced in his hand as it unwound until
it leapt into the street and began rolling away, and by the time Robert
seized it again it was still. He began to follow the thread, winding it back
around the spool as he walked.

The thread ran away from the houses of his friends, across streets
and through the narrow spaces between buildings, and soon Robert had
left the neighborhoods where he'd passed his life. He followed it through
empty city parks, past deserted corners, down alleys and in and out of
districts of warehouses and abandoned buildings. Finally the thread ran
up a wall, and when Robert climbed over he found himself standing in a
graveyard and, past the graves, there stood a small church. The thread
wound its way through the graves and up the side of the church to one of
the stained-glass windows. The window showed Saint Peter holding the
keys to the kingdom of heaven, and where the pupil of his right eye was
meant to be, a tiny chip of glass was missing, and the thread ran through
this hole and disappeared.

Robert walked between the headstones and hoisted himself up onto
the stone sill of the window. He put his eye to the hole in the saint's eye
and looked in. There had been a funeral in the church that day, and the
coffin on its bier was still before the altar. The coffin was open now, and
bent over it, feeding on the corpse inside with the greatest possible en-
joyment, was a vampire.

Now, Robert had heard people speak of vampires all his life, but this
was the first one he had ever seen. In his fear and revulsion he cried,
"Ugh," and the vampire straightened up. It was the handsome stranger.
He looked through the hole in Saint Peter's eye and saw Robert, and an
expression of such happiness and welcome came over his face that for a
moment Robert wanted to embrace him. Then he remembered what he
was looking at, and he dropped to the ground and ran out of the church-
yard, in terror that he'd hear the stranger's footsteps behind him. But no
one followed, and he reached his parents' house in safety.

All the next day he stayed in his room, but when evening came his parents insisted he go to the party. "You're young, this is the time for you to go to parties," his father said, and his mother added, "If you miss it, you'll regret it for the rest of your life." Robert went.

All of his friends were there, and the evil stranger was the last to arrive. The stranger danced, he told stories, he made everyone laugh, but all evening he kept his eye on Robert. When it came time for him to go, the stranger said, "Will Robert walk me out to the street?"

Robert didn't want to, but his best friend took him aside and said, "Why are you being such a baby? Walk out with him," and finally Robert agreed. They walked out to the street, and the stranger stood just outside the gate, Robert just inside. The stranger said, "Were you at the church last night?"

"No," Robert said.

"Did you see what I was doing?" the stranger asked.

Robert said, "No," shutting his eyes and shaking his head.

"Very well, then," the stranger said. "Tomorrow your mother will die." And he disappeared.

Robert went home. His mother was in the kitchen, drying the last of the dishes and humming part of a song that had been popular when she was a girl. When she saw him, her face filled with grief and she started to cry. "I don't understand," she sobbed. "We did everything we knew how for you. Where did we go wrong?" Robert didn't know what to say. She dropped the dish into the sink so it broke, and then she ran from the kitchen. In the morning, she was dead.

All day long Robert sat and mourned by the body of his mother. But when evening came his father called to him and said, "Go to the party," and wouldn't hear any answer but yes. And so Robert went.

Soon the evil stranger arrived and the rooms were filled with laughter, the music played more and more loudly, and the stranger kept his eye on Robert. When it was time for him to leave, he said, "Perhaps Robert will walk me out to the street."

Robert didn't want to, but his best friend took him aside and said, "You have to."

"Why?" Robert asked, but his friend didn't know and just pushed him toward the door.

They walked out to the street, and the stranger stood just outside the gate, Robert just inside. "Were you at the church the night before last?" he asked.

"No, I wasn't," Robert said, not looking at him.

"Did you see what I was doing?" the stranger persisted, but Robert just shook his head. "Very well," the stranger said. "Tomorrow your father will die." And he was gone.

Robert went home, where his father was reading the newspaper. When he looked up and saw Robert, his face went gray with loathing. "You're no son of mine," he roared. "Get out of my sight, you disgust me." Robert didn't know what to say to him. In the morning, his father was dead.

All day Robert mourned the loss of his parents, but when evening came he was afraid to be alone, so he dressed and went to the party. He tried to join in, but the stories his friends told seemed as meaningless as if they spoke in another language, and none of the young women wanted to dance with him. The evil stranger arrived. Soon everyone was whirling through the rooms of the house, shrieking with laughter. The stranger kept his eye on Robert, and when it was time to leave, he said, "Perhaps Robert will walk me out to the street."

"No," Robert said, but his best friend had just become engaged to be married, and he and his fiancée laughed happily and pushed him out the door. He walked with the stranger out to the street, and the stranger stood just outside the gate, Robert just inside.

"Were you at the church the other night?" the stranger demanded.

"No," Robert whispered.

"Did you see what I was doing?"

"No."

"Robert, think," the stranger said. "Are you certain?"

"Yes."

"Very well, then," the stranger sighed. "Tomorrow you yourself will die." And he vanished.

Robert didn't know where to go. But he remembered his grand-mother, and so he made his way across the city to her apartment.

It was late when he got there, but his grandmother had grown so old she no longer slept, and she let him into her parlor. They sat among the statues of the saints and the candles burning in their red glasses, and Robert told her what had happened. "And now I'm going to die, Nana," he said. "What can I do?"

His grandmother patted his leg. "You're going to have to die," she told him. "There's no other way. Now listen to me: when you're dead, you're not to be buried in the graveyard. You have to be buried at a cross-roads. And when they come to carry you out of the house, you can't be carried over the threshold. Have them dig a hole under the threshold and take you out through that."

"I don't understand, Nana," he said miserably.

"You're a good boy," she said, kissing him on the forehead. "Sleep here tonight."

In the morning Robert bought a coffin and brought it home with him. He wrote out the instructions for his burial just as his grandmother had told him and left some money he had with the note. Then he got into the coffin, lay down, and died.

It was difficult for the undertaker's men to dig a hole beneath the threshold of the house, and there was some trouble with the city's au-thorities about a burial at a crossroads, but Robert had left enough money, and everything was carried out according to his instructions.

Because it was a crossroads, each day people passed by in all direc-tions. One day a young man and his servant were walking together. The young man noticed a flower growing where the roads met. Now, the young man, whose name was Richard, loved flowers, and he had never seen one like this before. He said to his servant, "Go and pick that flower for me, I want it."

The servant laughed and said, "You'd better go pick it yourself."

So Richard went over to pick the flower. But when he got closer to it he saw that it was even more beautiful than he'd first thought, and so he very carefully uprooted it, took it to his home, and potted it. Richard was good with growing things, and the unusual flower flourished under his care. He kept it on the sill of a window where it received all the sunlight it needed, and he watered it and gently wiped the dust off its leaves with a damp cloth.

One morning Richard noticed that food was missing from the kitchen. At first he thought nothing of it, but when this had happened several days running he asked his servant if he were taking food. "Why would I sneak food in the middle of the night?" the servant replied. "There's someone new around here. You'd better keep an eye open." Richard resolved to wait up that night and see who was coming into the house and taking food.

When evening came, Richard and the servant concealed themselves behind a chair where they could watch the window. The moon rose. When its light touched the windowsill, the flower trembled, fell from its stem, and floated to the floor. As it touched the floor the flower turned into Robert, who quietly went into the kitchen and got himself something to eat. Now, Richard thought Robert was the most enchanting person he had ever seen. "Throw the plant away," the servant whispered, and Richard quickly went to the window, picked up the plant in its pot, and threw it out into the night as far as he could.

Robert finished eating. He came tiptoeing back to the window, and when he saw that the plant was gone, he didn't know what to do. Before he could think, Richard rushed out, caught him by the arms, and said, "I watered you and tended you. You've eaten my food. Stay here with me because I love you."

Robert, who had still been full of sleep from the time he'd spent as a flower, woke up completely and said, "Yes, I want to stay here."

So Robert and Richard lived together, and for a while their happiness was complete. One morning they went for a walk, not paying attention to where they were going, and their steps took them to a small church. "Come on," Richard said. "Let's go inside." The two of them walked up toward the door, when suddenly Robert stopped. There, seated on the sill under the stained-glass window of Saint Peter holding the keys to the kingdom of heaven, was the evil stranger. He spotted Robert immediately and fixed his eye on him. Richard saw nothing and went in, but the door closed behind him and when Robert tried it, it was locked. He turned away and ran off, and the evil stranger watched him go.

Robert went to his grandmother's apartment. She didn't seem surprised to see him. She let him into her parlor, and they sat there among the statues of the saints and the candles burning in their red glasses. "Nana," Robert moaned. "What can I do? I don't know how to rid myself of the evil stranger."

His grandmother smiled at him and patted his leg. "I can't tell you how to do that," she said.

Robert walked back to the church. The evil stranger saw him, and as Robert approached the door he leapt down from the windowsill and walked quickly over. "Were you at the church that night?" he asked.

"No," Robert said, trying to slip past him.

The stranger wouldn't let him pass. "Did you see what I was doing?" he persisted.

"No," Robert said, and he covered his face with his hands.

"Oh, Robert," the stranger said, shaking his head. "Very well. Tomorrow Richard will die."

"No," Robert cried, but he knew that saying "No" wouldn't have much effect on the stranger. And so, before he could disappear, Robert threw his arms around him. "I was in the church! I saw what you were doing!" he shouted as loudly as he could.

Now the stranger put his arms around Robert, and his embrace was so tight Robert couldn't have broken it no matter how hard he tried. "Then tell me," he said in Robert's ear. "Who am I?"

Robert pulled his head back and stared into the stranger's face until slowly his features became familiar. "Why, you're me," he said.

"Oh, thank you," the stranger, who was no longer a stranger, laughed. He kissed Robert once on the mouth and then dissolved in his embrace so that Robert was left hugging himself. Robert ran up to the door of the church, and it was open.

There had been a baptism in the church that day, and the font up at the front was still full of water. Richard was standing beside it, talking to two people. When Robert came up, he saw they were his parents, and though he was happy to see them again, he was shy and didn't know what to say to them. But he took Richard by the hand.

His mother said, "Robert, are you really happy this way?"

Robert looked at Richard, who was smiling at him. "Yes, I am," he said.

His father said, "Then this young man must be my son-in-law."

Robert smiled back at Richard. "Yes, he is," he said. From that time on Robert and Richard knew neither distress nor separation, and they lived together long and happily.

KING CROSSBILL

THERE WAS ONCE a young man named Christopher, who had a perfect nose, a dynamite smile, and hair so blond and wavy it was like sunlight shining on the sea. He was the handsomest young man in his village, and those villagers who'd seen something of the world swore he was the handsomest young man in anybody's village. Christopher had to agree—he was a knockout, no question about it, and the sighs of young women he passed in the street were like his theme song. Now it happened that many young men would also sigh when he passed. Though he didn't like to admit it—and therefore, never did—these were the sighs that sounded sweetest to his ear. Well, if Christopher didn't want to admit this to himself, he certainly saw no reason to let anyone else bring it to his attention, and he used his fists to change the topic of conversation whenever it came up. He also used his fists to discourage any young man who wanted to get past the sighing stage with him. It was a difficult position to maintain but the only one he felt comfortable in, and Christopher was determined to defend it. He got into a lot of fights.

Word of the handsome Christopher reached the ear of a powerful king, and one day there was a knock at Christopher's front door. It was the king, come round to see if what he'd heard were true. "Christopher,"

"King Thrushbeard," GB.

said the king, bestowing a smile on him worth a king's ransom. "Let me get right to the point. I'm looking for a companion, and I'm fairly certain you're him. Leave this village and come to my palace with me. We'll give each other the kind of life other people only live in their dreams." He was a handsome man himself, but even more distinguished than handsome, and even more good-humored than distinguished.

But Christopher, far from being swept off his feet, went white, then red, then black to have another man make him such a proposal—and right there on the front step, where anyone passing by could overhear. Of course, he couldn't knock down a king, though that was his first impulse, and because he'd never needed a second impulse before, he was at a loss as to what to do.

Just then a little red bird flew down under a pine tree in the front yard. It was that bird known as the red crossbill, which lives on the seeds inside pinecones. Now, pinecones are very difficult things to open, and the bird had developed a beak suitable to this task, with the top part curving in one direction and the bottom part curving in the other. Christopher pointed to the bird. "That's you," he growled. "King Crossbill." By which he meant that the bird's beak wasn't straight, and neither was the king. Then he slammed the door shut.

The king stood on the front step, watching the bird he'd been compared to as it pried apart the scales of a pinecone with its crooked beak. Then he said, "All right, Christopher," to the closed door, and went on his way.

Now, just about this time, Christopher's parents—with whom he lived—decided to sell the cottage and use the money to retire to someplace with a warmer climate. "We won't be able either to take you with us or to keep supporting you," they told him. "So we've decided to apprentice you to the first person who can teach you a trade."

A beggar happened to come to the door at that moment and overheard them. "Why not apprentice him to me?" the beggar suggested. His clothes were rags and tatters, but he looked as if he made up in wits what he lacked in wardrobe. "Mine is a very old and honorable profession, which flourishes no matter what state the economy is in. Consider for a moment: very few beggars ever become lawyers or stockbrokers, but a great many stockbrokers and lawyers become beggars." Well, this sounded reasonable to Christopher's parents, who anyway were a little tired of his conceited ways and all the fights he got into, and they thought begging might be just the thing for him. So they handed him over to the beggar with their blessing, sold their cottage, and off they went.

Christopher wasn't happy with the way things had turned out, but what could he do? Jobs were hard to come by, and surely the beggar would feed him. He accompanied the man out to the road, and they started walking. When they came to a crossroads, the beggar turned to him and said, "All right, Christopher. Let's see how well you can beg. Oh, but I'm forgetting—first you'll have to look like a beggar." And he made Christopher lie down in the dust and roll until his clothes were filthy and the gold of his hair was hidden. Then he withdrew behind an anise bush.

The first person who happened to come along the road was Christopher's best friend. "Jim," he said, stepping up to him with great confidence. "Jimmy, my man, I've gotten a job as a beggar. How about a little spare change?" But to Christopher's great surprise, his friend gave him nothing except a very dark frown, and walked past him.

The second person who came walking by was a young woman whose sighs over Christopher had always been of the deepest, most heartfelt sort. "Debbie," he said, putting all the charm in the world into her name. "I'm starting an exciting new career as a beggar. What about a little spare change for luck?" Debbie only wrinkled her nose as if there were an unpleasant odor, and continued on her way.

The third person traveling on that road was a young man who, not content merely to sigh over Christopher, had once asked him out on a date. Not being a king, he'd found himself knocked down by way of response. "Alex," said Christopher humbly. "I'm a beggar now. Can you spare any change?"

Well, Alex wasn't exactly thrilled to see him, but he didn't bear any resentment, either. He pulled a penny out of his pocket and gave it to Christopher. "Good luck," he said, and walked on.

The beggar came out from behind the anise bush. "A penny for your morning," he observed, taking the penny and pocketing it. "Not very impressive. Begging may be a little beyond your capabilities." The two of them set out on the road and walked long and long to the beggar's house.

On the way they passed through groves of orange trees. Christopher had never seen such glorious oranges, and he asked, "Whom do these groves belong to?"

"They belong to King Crossbill," the beggar answered, quite loudly, picking up the pace. Christopher walked more quickly to keep up with him. "These groves, and the groves beyond these, and the groves beyond those."

After a while they passed by a prosperous town. Christopher had never seen such snug, neat houses, and he asked, "Whom does this town belong to?"

"It belongs to King Crossbill," the beggar shouted, breaking into a run, and Christopher ran also to keep up with him. "This town, and the town beyond this, and the town beyond that."

They approached the edge of a forest that stretched from one edge of the world to the other. Christopher, who had never been fond of forests, asked, "Whom does this forest belong to?"

"It belongs to King Crossbill," howled the beggar. "And if this forest has an end, no one's ever seen it!" And with that, he snatched Christopher up under his arm and dashed into the forest like the north wind late for an appointment.

Christopher was carried deeper, and deeper, and even deeper than that into the forest. When the beggar finally set him down, they were standing before a hut abandoned among the trees. Moss embraced its walls, toadstools sprouted on the roof, and there was no glass in the windows, only spiderwebs. "Whom does this hut belong to?" Christopher asked unhappily, because he had already guessed the answer.

"Oh, this is mine," the beggar replied. "And yours, too—now."

"Could we have something to eat soon?" Christopher inquired, following him inside.

"Something to eat?" the beggar laughed in the darkness. "On that penny you earned? No, my friend, there's work for you to do here." He lit a candle stub. Christopher saw that the hut was filled with flowers, enormous bunches of them in white plastic buckets— everything that bloomed in gardens, in fields, or by the side of the road. "Since you're not much good as a beggar," the beggar continued, "we'll try you out on making flower arrangements. Then you'll have something to sell at the market."

"Flower arrangements?" snorted Christopher. "I don't think so. I'll chop firewood, or catch animals, or something. Flower arranging is effeminate."

"Effeminate?" the beggar cried in a terrible voice, making the walls tremble. He rolled up his sleeve and showed Christopher his right biceps, which was considerable. "Does this look effeminate to you?" Then he struck Christopher a blow to the mouth that knocked him across the room. "Now get to work," the beggar roared. "And those arrangements better be delicate, and dainty, and absolutely precious." And he gave Christopher a number of tiny rattan baskets shaped like bunnies and baby ducks in which to put the flowers. Christopher applied himself to the task as well as he was able.

Next morning he was sent off to market with his flower arrangements. He felt very self-conscious about selling them, and he didn't do well. Actually, he only sold one, and that was to a wealthy older gentleman who seemed undecided until Christopher, desperate to make a sale, smiled and made engaging small talk with him. The day passed, and when the market closed Christopher began packing up his merchandise. Just then a man in a hard hat and dirty work shirt swaggered by. He was very drunk and very large, and when he saw Christopher's goods, he lisped, "A flower boy! Isn't that just the sweetest little thing in the world?" He laughed uproariously, as if this were a particularly fine bit of humor. Then he knocked all the flower arrangements onto the ground and trampled them.

Christopher tried to stop him, but he was so dispirited that he wound up being lifted into the air and thrown several feet, then given a beating. He limped back to the beggar's hut with no flowers and only one sale in his pocket.

"Flowers a little too much for you, I see," the beggar observed. "Well, don't feel a complete loser. You'll be happy to know that I've gotten you a position at the king's castle. You're going to be a charwoman." Christopher was too tired and sore to ask if there wasn't an opening for a guard or a stable boy instead. He crept into a corner and fell asleep immediately.

In the morning he reported to the castle. He was given work scrubbing the floors, and as it was an enormous castle there were a great many floors to scrub. The other charwomen were all big powerful women in their fifties. They were very indignant to find Christopher among them. "Aren't you ashamed?" they demanded, standing around him in a circle, each with her big red fists firmly planted on her wide hips. "A big lump like you, doing women's work. Why don't you get a man's job?" They knocked over his bucket, swept dust kitties where he'd just finished scrubbing, and in general were very unpleasant coworkers. In fact, the only person who was at all nice was the pastry chef, who had taken a liking to him and brought him petit fours and a cup of cappuccino for his coffee break. He was very supportive.

"Don't let them ruffle your feathers," he told Christopher. "If you want to be a charwoman, honey, then you go right on out there and *be* a charwoman. Or a laundry woman. Or a milkmaid. *Go* for it." Christopher was very grateful for his kindness.

Well, with the pastry chef's encouragement, Christopher was able to persevere. He labored each day beside the other charwomen, scouring the floor of a different room. At night he took his earnings and whatever scraps of food he'd been given back to the beggar's hut. He couldn't help rebuking himself. "What a fool I was to reject King Crossbill," he mourned as he walked through the forest. "I could be living in a castle instead of cleaning one, and going home at night to someone who liked me instead of to the beggar, who never has anything pleasant to say." But there was nothing to be done about it.

One morning when he showed up at the castle, Christopher was told that there was to be a grand ball that night. As the other charwomen were all needed elsewhere, he would have to polish the entire black-and-white marble floor of the ballroom himself. He set to work immediately, but the ballroom was so vast that it seemed he'd never be able to get it all cleaned. The pastry chef, busy in the kitchen, was unable to come by with snacks and gossip, so Christopher completely lost track of the time. When he finally finished buffing the last white marble square in the furthest corner, the chandeliers suddenly lit up, the great French doors of the ballroom swung open, and the guests began to make their arrivals.

Beautiful women in glittering gowns walked in arm in arm, and handsome men in tuxedos kissed one another hello; handsome women in tuxedos kissed one another hello, and beautiful men in glittering gowns walked in arm in arm. Everyone was so happy to see everyone else, and the delighted laughter rose and fell, rose and fell. Musicians played, and tall slim glasses of champagne were passed around. Christopher stood in the corner, watching it all and longing to join in. To his chagrin he recognized Alex—Alex, whom he'd knocked down, Alex, who'd given him a penny when he was begging, Alex, who it seemed was a guest of honor here, hugged and kissed and greeted by everyone. Then the king made his entrance.

Oh, he was a handsome man in his velvet and silk and his gold crown, but he was even more distinguished than he was handsome, and more good-humored than distinguished. Christopher lost his heart to him between the end of one second and the start of the next. "I would give anything," he murmured forlornly to himself, "to be the guest of that king." At that moment the king turned toward him, and he saw that it was none other than King Crossbill. How Christopher wanted to lift up one of the black marble squares and disappear beneath it with his rags, his dirt-filled hair, and his wash-bucket hands. But it was too late. King Crossbill had seen him and was striding across the room, holding out his arms and smiling.

"Don't be afraid," he said as he took Christopher's hands in his. "I'm the beggar you were apprenticed to. I'm the man who bought your flowers, and I'm the construction worker who trampled them. I'm the pastry chef who encouraged you when no one else would give you a kind word. I did this because I love you and because I saw how much you would need to learn before you finally came out."

Christopher couldn't meet his eyes. "I've been a coward and the slave of fear all my life," he said in a low voice. "Maybe a hut in the forest is the best place for someone like me."

"My dear friend," King Crossbill laughed, putting his arm around Christopher's shoulders. "You've been apprenticed to me, and your apprenticeship has only started." And he led him out into the room to meet the other guests.

BEAUTY AND THE BEAST

T HERE WAS ONCE a very prosperous and therefore much respected merchant who had three sons. The oldest cared for nothing but power and wanted to rule the world. The next oldest was in love with brutality and was never so happy as when he was destroying something or someone, preferably with his hands. Their names were Bradley and Brian, and the merchant couldn't have been prouder of them. His youngest son was a different matter entirely. He didn't seem to have very much drive, he always did as he was told, and he had an embarrassing fondness for flowers, which were not a commodity the merchant traded in. His name was Buddy, but because, as even his father had to admit, he was much prettier than boys usually are, everyone called him Beauty. It wasn't meant as a compliment.

One day the merchant called his sons together. "Boys," he announced, "I have to be away on business for a couple of days, and I want you to keep an eye on my affairs while I'm gone. What do you want me to bring you from my trip?"

"A handgun in a velvet case," Bradley said.

"Kid leather boxing gloves with about five pounds of lead in each one," Brian said.

"Belinda and the Monster" and "Grattula-Bedattula," IF; "Beauty and the Beast," PCFT.

"That's fine, boys," the merchant nodded. "Beauty, what about you?"

Beauty shrugged. "I don't know. Maybe a flower, if you see an interesting one." It was what Beauty always asked for, though so far he'd never been brought one.

"Hmmph," said the merchant, which was what he always said. He tossed his briefcase in the back of his car and drove off. No sooner was he out of sight than Bradley and Brian went into his study. Brian forced the lock of the drawer where the merchant kept his private papers, and Bradley eagerly began going through them.

"This is men's work," they told Beauty. "You go make us some coffee." And because Beauty wanted nothing so much as to be accepted by his brothers, he did as he was told.

A few days passed. The merchant closed his deals in a profitable manner and was driving home. He had a handgun for Bradley and boxing gloves for Brian, but there had been no flowers in the boardrooms where he'd attended his meetings, only a few dusty philodendrons, and so he brought nothing for Beauty. The merchant came to a road he didn't recall seeing before, which looked like it ran toward home in a much more direct way than the one he was on. "What's time if not money?" he said to himself, and he pulled onto it. But the road gave a turn, and then another, and soon the merchant found himself among canyons and pine trees. He drove the rest of the day without seeing another car, or a house, or a jogger. Evening came and he had to drive more slowly, because the road was unlit. Suddenly his headlights dimmed and the car stopped. He tried his cellular phone, but that was dead as well. Swearing to himself to keep up his spirits, he locked his car and started to walk.

Well, he walked, and he walked, and he walked a little more, and just when he'd reached the point where he couldn't take another step to save his life and couldn't bear the thought of going back the way he'd come, he saw a light up ahead. He made his way to it and soon came to a condominium. There were no cars parked around it, and though the lobby was brightly lit, no other lights shone in the building. He walked up to the door. It was unlocked and he stepped into the lobby. "Hello?" he called, but there was no security guard, no receptionist, no manager to be found. All there was in the lobby was an elevator. The merchant looked inside it. There were only two buttons, one marked "Lobby" and the other "Penthouse." So he pushed the button for the penthouse. The doors closed, and up he rose.

When the doors opened again, the merchant stepped out into the largest, most luxurious penthouse he'd ever seen. It was well furnished but not overly well furnished, and when, with a practiced eye, he priced some of the antiques and the art on the walls, he was truly astonished at the lack of any security system. "Hello?" he called. "Is anyone home?" But it seemed no one was. Then he sniffed the air and followed his nose to a dining table that was set for dinner, and when he lifted the lids off the chafing dishes, he was amazed to discover that someone liked all the same things he did. "Well," he said to himself. "A little something to eat wouldn't do me any harm." So he sat down at the head of the table and helped himself to a little of this and a little of that. He ate, and he ate, and he ate until he couldn't possibly swallow another mouthful, and then he had just a little more, because it would be a sin to waste good food.

When he was finally finished he got up. He didn't see a phone anywhere, and this didn't really surprise him because there were no lights in the penthouse, only forests of candles. He walked back over to the elevator, but the doors had closed and no matter where he looked he couldn't find a call button. "Someone's bound to come home sooner or later," he reasoned with himself. "The best thing I can do is make myself comfortable." There was a fireplace with a good fire roaring away in it, and in front of the fire a well-upholstered leather couch waited. "Just the thing," the merchant said, testing it for softness, and in no time he was sound asleep.

When he woke, it was morning. The fire had burned down to embers and he had been covered with a fur rug. "Hello?" he called. "Has anyone come home?" But it didn't seem that anyone had. On the other hand, the table that had held dinner the night before was now groaning beneath breakfast, and yes, when he checked, the merchant found everything just the way he liked it. "After the day I had yesterday," he told himself as he sat down, "breakfast could only do me good." He ate until he thought he would burst, and then, because there were many areas of the world where people didn't have enough food, he ate just a tiny bit more. Just as he was finishing his last cup of coffee, the elevator doors opened.

No one was in the elevator. Still, the merchant couldn't spend the rest of his life in the penthouse, so he put his suit jacket on and stepped toward the elevator. Just as he was about to get in, he noticed something he hadn't seen the night before. Next to the elevator stood a small lacquer table on which was a bowl, and growing in the bowl was an orchid. Its blossom was black and blue, and the merchant didn't much care for its sweet heavy scent, but he remembered his son Beauty's request. "What could it hurt?" he asked himself, and because he couldn't think of any answer to that he broke off the flower and put it in his pocket.

Well, there must have been a security system after all, because an alarm suddenly went off that sounded like the roar of an angry animal. Then a door burst open, and someone huge pounded into the room. The merchant was seized by the front of his jacket and slammed into the wall. "Aren't you a sweetheart?" snarled the huge someone. "I give you shelter, food, a warm fire, and you show your gratitude by stealing from me. I'm going to enroll you in a little workshop I teach, 'How to Be the Perfect Guest.' "

Now, the huge irritated someone was wearing nothing except a costume made of leather straps and steel rings. Because the merchant had seen harnesses like that only on horses and dogs, he concluded that he was in the grip of a Beast.

But he remained calm. "You have every right to be upset," he said soothingly. "My behavior was unthinkable. Let me make it up to you."

"What do you have in mind?" the Beast growled.

The merchant reached into the inner pocket of his jacket and pulled out his checkbook and pen. "Name your price," he said grandly.

"Money?" the Beast howled. "Look around, sugar. Does it look like I need money?" He lifted the merchant into the air and gave him a shake that loosened all his bones.

Now the merchant was truly frightened. "Don't kill me," he begged as he dangled. "Please, I have a family to support. My poor boys, Bradley, Brian, Beauty—"

"Beauty?" the Beast repeated. He slowly lowered the merchant back down to the floor. "You have a son named Beauty?" He thought about it for a moment, smoothing the shoulders of the merchant's jacket. "Well, I'll tell you what we're going to do. You're going to keep the orchid, and when you get home you're going to send me this son of yours named Beauty." The Beast straightened the merchant's tie, sliding the knot up so high that the merchant couldn't breathe. "I know I can trust you in this matter," he whispered, then gave the merchant a playful little shove that sent him flying into the elevator. The doors closed, and down he went.

When he got to the lobby, he was already running. He found his car parked just outside the door and didn't stop to wonder how it got there; he just jumped in, revved the engine, and took off in a shriek of tires. He made it home in record time, and once there gave Bradley and Brian their gifts and sent them away. Then he turned to Beauty. "I brought you something," he said, pulling the orchid out of his pocket.

"Oh, an orchid!" Beauty exclaimed, and then he frowned. "What a strange one—it looks like a bruise." But when he lifted it to his nose and inhaled, the sweetness overwhelmed him. "Oh, thank you, Father. It's heaven."

"Yes, well, I went to a little bit of trouble to get it for you," the merchant said, and then, keeping his eyes focused on something else, he told

Beauty what had befallen him in the Beast's condominium. "So you see, Beauty," he concluded, "none of this would have happened if you hadn't insisted on a flower instead of something more sensible, like your brothers. Now, I think it only right that you take a little responsibility for your actions, and go and take my place in the Beast's penthouse." And he glanced at Beauty to see how he was taking this.

Well, Beauty knew that he was a disappointment to his father, and he'd always tried to make up for it by doing whatever the merchant told him. This time was no exception. "Very well," he agreed sadly. "I'll go pack a suitcase."

So the merchant drove Beauty to the lonely condominium and said good-bye to him. Before Beauty had even reached the door, the merchant, who found good-byes painful, was gone in a cloud of dust. Beauty walked through the lobby and into the elevator. He pressed the button marked "Penthouse." The doors closed, and up he rose.

It was still daylight in the penthouse, though it had been dusk down in the lobby, and no one seemed to be about. Everything was just as the merchant had described it, but because Beauty wasn't hungry there was no food on the dining table. There was nothing to do, so he set his suitcase down and looked around, and though the antiques and artwork didn't really interest him, there were orchids everywhere. He didn't realize how much time had passed until suddenly all the candles flamed up at the same time, a door opened, and someone came in. Beauty recognized the Beast from the merchant's description of him, but just to make sure, he asked, "Are you the Beast?"

"Yes," the Beast rumbled. "And you're Beauty. The jerk who tried to steal my orchid sent you to me to save his own skin. Not that it or anything inside it is worth saving." The merchant was a very well-respected member of the community, and Beauty had never heard him spoken of in this way. It made him feel funny. "During the day," the Beast went on, "you'll have the place to yourself, and your only responsibility will be to take care of my orchids for me. I've got a lot of them, and they're not doing so well. At night, after you've eaten, your only responsibility will be to make me happy. Do you understand?"

"Yes," Beauty said.

"Good. Follow me." The Beast led the way to a huge bedroom, such as Beauty had never been in before—something like a luxury dungeon. "Get out of your clothes," the Beast said. "Let's have a look at you." Beauty, who was used to doing what he was told, undressed. "You're a little skinny," the Beast observed. "But you'll do. I'm going to train you to please me. I'm tough, but I'm fair: if you do your best, we'll get along fine. If you don't, you'll be disciplined. Now get over here, it's time for your first lesson." So Beauty went over, and though the Beast was demanding and thorough, he wasn't cruel, and Beauty had a much better time than he thought he would. When they were finished, the Beast asked an odd question. "Beauty," he said, "do you love me?"

"That was incredible," Beauty said earnestly. "But no, I don't love you. How could I? You're a Beast." The Beast seemed to accept this answer, and left. Beauty took a shower and went to sleep.

The next morning he began his exploration of the penthouse. It proved to be much larger than he expected; in fact, if there had been even one more room, it would have been endless. Behind one door he found an artist's studio, behind another a mechanic's workshop, while another and another and another door opened on a confectioner's kitchen, a fortune-teller's parlor, and an assayer's office full of mineral samples. In short, he found every conceivable occupation and interest there in the Beast's penthouse. And in each room he entered, Beauty discovered orchids. They were all the colors of the rainbow—red like the welts left by a belt, blue like fresh bruises, yellow like bruises that have begun to fade—but all gave out the same sweet heavy fragrance. A few were doing well, most suffered from poor drainage or not enough water, were root bound or covered with dust. It seemed to Beauty he'd been given an endless task.

When evening came and the candles all caught flame at the same moment, he went to the dining table and found his favorite supper, peanut-
butter-and-datenut-bread sandwiches and sparkling water. He ate, and
just as he finished, a door opened and the Beast came out from wherever
he spent the daylight hours. Beauty went with him to the bedroom for
his second lesson, which ended as the first had, with the Beast asking,
"Beauty, do you love me?" and Beauty answering him, "No."

The days passed. One afternoon, roaming with his spray bottle,
Beauty opened a door and found himself in a library. Now, he had never
cared very much for books, associating them with his brother Bradley's
dreary quest for power. But on a little table, beside an orchid infested
with spider mites, he noticed a book entitled *The Care and Feeding of Orchids*. It was just what he needed. He sat down in a comfortable wing-
backed chair and read the book from cover to cover. Beauty not only
discovered that orchids do best in an enclosed controlled environment,
such as a greenhouse, but that he really enjoyed reading. In the weeks
that followed, he browsed the bookcases, reading up on every subject
that presented itself to him.

Another day he opened a door that revealed a fully equipped gymna-
sium, filled with Nautilus machines and Stairmasters and racks of
chromium free-weights. Now, Beauty had never been greatly taken with
exercise of any kind, because it seemed linked to his brother Brian's brutality. But beside an orchid that was getting far too much direct sunlight
lay a book called *Building the Body of Beauty*, and its silver-toned pho-
tographs revealed to him that exercise could increase the body's aes-
thetic appeal. And if greater strength and endurance went along with it,
well, maybe that wasn't so bad. He read through the book and began to
work out on a daily basis.

Meanwhile, the Beast was keeping his eye on Beauty, though Beauty
wasn't aware of it. As Beauty's strength increased, the Beast encouraged
him to put up greater resistance in their nightly sessions. And afterward,

as they lay back together, the Beast would engage him in conversation about whatever subject Beauty happened to be reading, whether it was philosophy, color theory, or French pastry techniques. But every conversation ended in the same way, with the Beast asking, "Beauty, do you love me?" and Beauty answering, "No."

As his workout program, which came to include swimming, aerobics, yoga, and Tai Chi as well as weight lifting, and his reading (he'd drawn up a list of the two thousand most influential books in the world and was working his way through them) began to make greater demands on his time, Beauty thought it would be more practical if the Beast's orchids were gathered together in one location. He decided to build a greenhouse out on the terrace, with a humidifying system and a thermostat so the orchids could be kept in as perfect an environment as possible. In the penthouse he found the workshops and materials needed for every stage of the project, and Beauty, who'd never attempted anything on this scale— or any other scale, for that matter—set to work with great excitement.

In the evenings he showed blueprints and diagrams to the Beast, and the two of them discussed each and every point. Frequently they disagreed, because Beauty was developing his own opinions for the first time in his life. Sometimes they even came to blows, but they always came together. Beauty taught himself carpentry and glaziery, electrical engineering and thermodynamic theory, until one late afternoon in the middle of summer there was a greenhouse on the terrace, and every orchid the Beast had was inside. The scent was like the outskirts of heaven.

It had been a very hot day, and when Beauty sat down at the dining room table for supper he didn't want more than a salad and a little light consommé. As he lifted a spoonful of the soup to his lips, the late sunlight suddenly sparkled in it, and in the light he saw his father's face. The merchant looked years older and much diminished, as if he were being dined on from inside by some terrible worry. "Of course," Beauty cried, setting the spoon back down in his bowl. "He doesn't know what's become of me. He probably thinks I'm dead and that it's his fault." He determined to ask the Beast for permission to visit his father.

That night they had a heated discussion over the proper temperature setting for the greenhouse. Beauty prevailed, quoting all the authorities on the subject, but lost the ensuing wrestling match, though the Beast noted with approval how difficult it was becoming to subdue him. When Beauty had admitted defeat and finished his penalty, he turned to the Beast and said, "There's something I need to ask you."

"Ask," the Beast replied, watching him.

"I saw my father today in a spoonful of soup," Beauty told him. "He looked terrible, and I think he's worried about me. Will you let me go visit him and tell him everything's all right?"

"No," said the Beast.

"I need to see him," Beauty stated. "I'm not going to stay away long—I like it here. Now give me your permission."

The Beast saw that Beauty was determined to have his way, and this pleased him. But he said in his gruffest voice, "You want to go, then go. You can have three days. But if you're not back here by sundown on the fourth day, don't bother coming back at all, because none of this will be here for you."

"I promise," Beauty swore. "Thank you."

"Now there's something I need to ask you," the Beast said. "Beauty, do you love me?"

Beauty was grateful to the Beast for giving him permission and as happy in the penthouse as he'd ever been anywhere—happier, actually. He almost said, "Yes," but then thought, Why should I lie to him? "No," he said. The Beast nodded, bid him good night, and left.

Next morning the elevator doors were open. Beauty stepped inside, pressing the lobby button; the doors closed, and down he went. He crossed the silent lobby and had just put his hand to the glass door when he heard the Beast say behind him, "Remember: be back here by sundown on the fourth day, or none of this will be here for you." Beauty looked over his shoulder, eager to see the Beast by the light of day, but there was no one there. When he turned back to the door, he saw it was the front door of his father's house. He opened it and went inside.

At that hour of the morning, he knew, his father would be having coffee in his study and going over the books. But when Beauty entered the study, he found Bradley sitting behind the merchant's desk, examining the accounts, and Brian lying on the floor, cracking walnuts between his fingers. "Hi," Beauty said. "Where's Father?"

"Well, look who's here," said Bradley, not looking up.

"Where's Father?" Beauty asked again, this time in the tone of voice he used when he and the Beast were in disagreement over some point of conversation.

Bradley glanced at him in surprise. "Out in the garden," he answered, and scowled.

Beauty turned to leave, and Brian, as he often used to when Beauty was living at home, made kissing noises at his back. Without thinking, Beauty gave him a look the Beast had often given him, something like a stone wall pushed into the other person's eyes. Brian quickly busied himself with his walnuts.

The merchant was sitting on a bench under a willow tree in the furthest corner of the garden, his hands clasped between his knees, his head hanging. He looked years older. "Father," Beauty cried. "There's no need to worry, I'm fine. See, I've come back to visit you."

The merchant looked up at him and blinked. "Have you been away?" he asked.

"You dropped me off at the Beast's condominium," Beauty reminded him, "and left me there. Haven't you been worrying yourself sick about what happened to me?"

"No, not really," replied the merchant.

"Then what on earth's the matter with you?" Beauty demanded.

"Your brothers," the merchant whined miserably. "They've taken the business away from me. I was too old, they said. Too old to run my own business that I started from nothing."

Beauty was quickly losing patience with his father. But the old man looked so lost that he sat down beside him on the bench. Now, one of the subjects that he and the Beast talked about in bed happened to be business law. After carefully questioning the merchant, Beauty discovered that his father hadn't actually signed anything over to his sons but had merely been intimidated by them. He took his father by the arm and gently escorted him to the study, closing the door behind them. Twenty minutes later, the door opened again, and Bradley and Brian slunk out, dispossessed of the family business. The merchant sat behind his own desk, once again the man he had been. "I don't know what that Beast has done to you, son," he declared, "but I could use a man like you at my side. Stay here now, and I'll make you my partner."

His father's words would have once given Beauty the greatest happiness, but now he shook his head. "No," he said, not unkindly. "I'm just visiting. I have to get back to the Beast by sunset three days from now, or everything I've got going there will disappear." But to show the merchant that he appreciated the offer, Beauty gave him some tips on how to safeguard his business against any future takeover attempts.

Bradley, who had been listening at the keyhole, straightened up and said in a low voice, "We really have to plan something special for our little brother, to show him how grateful we are for everything he's done."

"Yeah," agreed Brian, making a fist of one hand and punching it into the other.

On the evening of the third day, as Beauty was preparing early for bed, there was a knock on his bedroom door and in came his brothers. They had a magnum of champagne, already opened, and three glasses. "So you're going back tomorrow," Bradley observed wistfully. "Look,

Brian and I are both sorry there's been so much bad blood between us. Can we have a drink together and let bygones be bygones?"

"Oh, of course we can," Beauty said, taking a glass. He had dreamed more times than he could remember of his brothers saying something like this to him.

Bradley poured three drinks, then held his own glass out and said, "Here's to your alternative lifestyle: may it bring you all the happiness in the world." They all touched glasses. Beauty threw his head back and drank, not noticing that his brothers tossed the contents of their own glasses over their shoulders. Bradley poured again. "Here's to the three of us," he toasted, "brothers forever." Beauty drank to that as well. "Here's to old times," pledged Bradley, and Beauty drank. Then Brian made a toast, "Here's to us on top and you on the bottom, where you belong." But Beauty didn't drink to that, because the sleeping potion Bradley had put in the champagne was very potent, and Beauty was unconscious.

He didn't wake up until late the following day. His head throbbed, his stomach felt queasy, and he didn't remember anything. He thought perhaps something to eat might at least settle his stomach, and made his way down to the kitchen. All he felt like was a little light consommé, so he opened a can and heated some up. It was sunset, and as he lifted a spoonful of soup to his lips the light of the setting sun danced in it, and in the light he saw the Beast's face. His head cleared and he remembered what day it was. He dropped his spoon and ran for the front door. As he reached it, Bradley and Brian appeared, blocking his way, their faces stony with dislike. "Oh, you're not leaving yet, little brother," Bradley informed him. "Not until we're absolutely certain it's too late."

"Yeah," agreed Brian, folding his big arms across his chest.

"You're in my way," roared Beauty, and with a flick of each wrist he sent Bradley flying in one direction and Brian flying in the other. He threw open the door and rushed out. By the time he'd taken two steps, he realized he would never return to the merchant's house; by the time he took the third step, he was entering the lobby of the Beast's condominium. The elevator doors were open. Beauty pressed the button, the doors closed, and up he rose.

Although it was almost night down below, up in the penthouse it was still broad daylight. Beauty raced from room to room to room, calling for the Beast, but room after room after room was empty. At last he thought to check the greenhouse, and entered it. In his absence, every orchid had bloomed. In their midst, silent, waiting in the intoxicating scent, stood the Beast. "You're still here," laughed Beauty. "Oh, I'm so glad! I love you!" Then it occurred to him that he was finally seeing the Beast by the light of day. He took a good long look. To his amazement, the person standing before him wasn't a beast at all, but the handsomest man he had ever seen. "Beast," he said in bewilderment. "Were you under a spell all this time?"

"No," answered the Beast. "You were. Now the spell is broken, and you're free. You can leave or stay—you can do anything you want."

"I want to stay with you," Beauty said, and then he smiled. "On one condition."

"What's the condition?" the Beast asked.

"That tonight, after dinner," Beauty replied, "you'll be Beauty, and I'll be the Beast."

"Anything you want," the Beast promised him. And as Beasts do, he kept his word.

HANSEL AND GRETEL

THERE WERE ONCE two children who lived with their parents in a cottage on the edge of the Great Forest, and their parents treated them badly. Who knows why? Perhaps the parents had been badly treated by their own parents and were continuing a family tradition; perhaps the parents hadn't meant to have children at all and would have been happier with a cat. It was all the same to the children—sometimes they were neglected, sometimes abused.

The girl, whose name was Gretel, had both eyes open and knew how to take care of herself. When there was a storm coming in the little cottage, she knew it and kept out of the way. As a consequence of this she was more neglected than abused. But the boy, whose name was Hansel, was dreamy and withdrawn, and the only protection he had from trouble was to lose himself in daydreams and old movie magazines, which wasn't always helpful. And so he was more abused than neglected.

The brother and sister loved each other very much, and though they had no other companions, they were content and often quite happy. Gretel, neglected by their parents, was glad to feel needed by her brother, and Hansel was grateful to have someone look out for him.

"Hansel and Gretel," AL; "The Lost Children," BBFF; "Hansel and Gretel," GB; "The Garden Witch," IF.

One night, when the moon wasn't shining and everyone was asleep, the mother sat up in bed, opened one eye, and said, "It's time to get rid of the children."

The father sat up beside her, opened one eye and said, "I think you may be right. How?"

The mother stared into the dark long and hard. Finally she said, "We'll take them into the forest and leave them there."

The father said, "Good idea." Then they both closed their eyes and lay back down, and when they woke up in the morning neither of them remembered their conversation.

But the father looked out the window. Black clouds stampeded across the sky, and the wind moaned like someone who had just received terrible news. "What a nice day," observed the father. "Let's take the children for a walk in the woods."

"Why, that's a wonderful idea," the mother said. "I'll pack a lunch."

The father went to the children and told them to get ready because they were all going to go for a walk. Gretel immediately knew something was wrong, because they never did anything as a family. She took her brother outside. "Fill your pockets with white pebbles," she told him.

"How come?" Hansel wanted to know.

"They're taking us for a walk," she told him. "I think they're going to try to lose us." So Hansel stuffed his pockets full.

When lunch was packed—which didn't take long—the family set out into the forest. Soon they were deep among the trees. Hansel, who hated the forest, grew even more withdrawn than usual. Gretel held his hand. Every few steps she whispered, "Now," and Hansel would drop a pebble.

When they had walked for quite a while, the parents sat Hansel and Gretel down side by side on a fallen tree. "Children, your mother and I are going to gather some firewood," the father said.

"You wait right here for us," the mother said. "Here's your lunch. Don't eat it right away." Then the parents turned around, and by the time they had taken ten steps they had forgotten that they even had children, and thought they were in the forest to gather firewood. So they picked up a few sticks and carried them back to their cottage.

When they were out of sight, the children stood and walked over to where the last of the white pebbles lay. The stones ran back through the forest, glowing faintly in the gloom under the trees, all the way to their parents' cottage. "Should we go back?" Hansel wondered.

"I don't think so," Gretel said. "Let's see what they gave us for lunch."

All they found inside the paper bag was a candy bar. Gretel didn't have much of a sweet tooth. But of all the things Hansel wanted and rarely got, it seemed that a little sweetness was what he got least often. He ate his half of the candy bar happily, and then, because he knew she wouldn't mind, ate Gretel's half as well. Then they took each other by the hand and set off, with their backs turned on the direction they'd come from.

They were in the Great Forest, which is also known as the Endless Forest if you happen to be lost in it, as anyone who'd ever been lost there could tell you, if you could ever find someone who'd ever been lost there and had found his way out. But those people are few and far between, because the trees grow very close together there, and the leaves overhead aren't inclined to let much light get through, and while most directions lead deeper into the forest, very few lead out of it.

The children walked all day until the gloom slowly turned to complete blackness, and those animals that wake up and look for their dinner in the dark began to do so. Hansel was very nervous, and though Gretel told him everything would be all right, she began to grow a little apprehensive herself.

Suddenly they saw a light up ahead of them, shining between the trunks of the trees. They made their way toward it as quickly as they could and finally came into a little clearing. There they found a circle of spotlights on tall black stands, and within that a circle of movie cameras on dollies, their film running, though there wasn't a cameraman to be seen. But most amazing of all was the little house in the middle of the clearing, which the lights lit and the cameras filmed, because that little house was made entirely of candy.

"Candy!" Hansel exclaimed, and he ran out in front of the cameras, right up to the house, and broke off a piece of it. "Chocolate-covered caramel," he cried, and began to eat as fast as he could. Gretel, who would have preferred something hot, approached with a certain hesitation. "We can stay here," Hansel said with his mouth full, "forever!"

"Well," Gretel began doubtfully, but that was as far as she got, because at that moment the macadamia-nut-brittle front door opened, and a lady came out.

Oh, she was beautiful! She had big bouffant hair the color of moonlight and a wrap of white fur, and when the lights hit her long dress they broke into a thousand pieces and danced. She wasn't young at all, and her face had long ago been marked by heartbreak and tragedy, the way long ago the desert was mistreated by the ocean. The lady didn't even glance at Gretel but looked deep into Hansel's eyes and said, "*You*," as if he were the one she'd always been waiting for. She had a voice like cigarette smoke, like black silk stockings, like staying up late every night.

"Yes," Hansel agreed, and he forgot about eating.

"Come in," the lady invited. "Everything's ready." And Hansel walked into the cottage. Then the lady glanced at Gretel and her face changed, as if Gretel had just said something funny. "Not much to look at, are you, honey?" she said. "But you'd better come inside, too. It's going to get cold out here." Gretel didn't like the lady, but she went in after her brother.

She didn't like the inside of the house, either. It's true, it wasn't made of candy like the outside, but the dimness and the dust and the clutter made her uncomfortable. A cigarette burning in an ashtray was about to fall off onto a little table, and Gretel put it out. "Leave things the way they are, honey," the lady said. "Everything's just the way I like it." Then she turned back to Hansel and said in her magic voice, the one she used only for him, "Come and talk to me."

Hansel followed her through the cottage, which was much, much larger on the inside than on the outside, to the lady's dressing room. Her beautiful dresses hung in the closet like sleeping angels, and the lady sat down at a table in front of three mirrors. "Make yourself comfortable," she said. "Tell me about yourself."

Hansel sat in a little armchair piled with cushions. "Who *are* you?" he asked, and the lady laughed. It was an enchanting laugh, and Hansel wished more than anything that he could laugh that way.

"We're going to be friends," the lady told him. "Do you like magic?" And without waiting for an answer, she opened a jar of cream, smoothed some on her face, and wiped it off with tissue. "Now," she said. "Who shall I be?" She took out pencils and brushes and tiny pots of color, and with just a few strokes she gave herself a completely different face, one Hansel was sure he had seen in either his movie magazines or his daydreams. "Would you like to learn how to do this?" she asked.

"Oh, yes," Hansel breathed. "Do you think I could?"

The lady moved over and patted the place next to her on the little bench, and Hansel came and sat beside her. She put her pencils to his eyes, and then her brushes, and when Hansel looked in the three mirrors he had eyes just like hers. He was very happy. "I have so many secrets to tell you," the lady confided, and in the days that followed, Hansel learned them all.

Gretel, meanwhile, had nothing to do. The one thing she could think of—straightening up some of the clutter the lady lived in—was forbidden to her. She only had to wipe the dust off a table with her finger for the lady to appear, saying, "Leave it alone, honey. Everything's already the way I like it." More than anything, Gretel missed feeling needed by her brother, who spent all his time with the lady. Gretel saw that he changed day by day, and it seemed to her that the lady was eating Hansel a little bit at a time.

One afternoon, when the children had been living in the cottage for much longer than she liked, Gretel came upon Hansel, seated in front of the three mirrors, experimenting with the brushes and little pots of color. The lady was nowhere in sight. "We have to escape," Gretel said urgently.

"What do you mean?" Hansel asked, concentrating on the line he was drawing on one of his eyelids.

Gretel looked into the middle mirror and saw that her brother had the lady's eyes. "She's turning you into her," she said unhappily.

"No, not really," Hansel said. "She's teaching me how to be a star." He leaned back and looked at himself in the mirror. It seemed to him that the person who looked back at him was stronger and more beautiful than anything Hansel had ever been afraid of. He said, "Tonight she's going to tell me the secret of how to walk in heels. I can't leave now." Then the lady came in and sat next to him on the bench, and Gretel couldn't talk to him anymore.

She knew that it was up to her to rescue her brother. Now, Gretel had been watching, and she saw that the lady had only one weakness, which was her vanity. To tell the truth, it was really more of an appetite than a weakness, because in the evenings, while the children had their supper, the lady never ate anything. Instead, she lived on the attention and admiration that she got from Hansel. Brooding on this, Gretel made her plans.

On the day Gretel decided to escape from the cottage, she went into the kitchen, removed all the racks from the oven, and began cleaning them as quickly as she could. She'd no sooner started than the lady appeared, saying, "Leave that alone, honey. Everything's already the way I like it."

"Oh, I'm sorry, I forgot," Gretel said. Then she widened her eyes as if she were seeing the lady for the first time and said, "Why, you're a movie star, aren't you?"

Now, it's hard to say exactly what the lady was, but she had certainly been a movie star in her time, and in fact, she had been several. So she said, "Yes. Yes, I suppose I am." She smiled at Gretel, which she hadn't done before.

"In fact," Gretel went on, "you starred in my favorite movie of all time."

"Really?" the lady marveled, and suddenly she spoke in the magic voice she used for Hansel. "Which one was it?"

"*The Queen in the Oven*," Gretel said. "I saw it five times. You were brilliant in it." She crossed her fingers, hoping her plan would work.

Now, the lady had been the star of a lot of movies, but for the life of her she couldn't remember having been in *The Queen in the Oven* or even having heard of it before. But she couldn't resist Gretel's praise, so she said, "Oh, yes. That was a very demanding role," and waited to hear more about it.

"Do you know my favorite scene?" Gretel asked. "It still gives me goosebumps. It's the final scene, where the enemy soldiers have broken into the castle, and you flee into the kitchen."

"The kitchen," the lady repeated, visualizing it.

"Hopelessly outnumbered, your kingdom in flames, you choose death before dishonor," Gretel said.

"Yes," the lady declared, caught up in the story now.

"The oven door is open. Without hesitation, you climb into it," Gretel said, keeping her eyes on the lady, and she began humming something tragic but tempestuous.

"Of course," the lady cried, enjoying herself thoroughly. "My funeral pyre, and my monument!" She even went so far as to climb into the oven, calling, "Farewell!"

As soon as she was inside, Gretel slammed the door shut, jammed a chair under the handle so it couldn't open, and turned the oven up as high as it would go. Then she ran to find Hansel.

He was sitting in front of the triple mirror in one of the lady's long sparkling dresses, choosing a wig for himself because his own hair was still so short. He had decided on one that was his own hair color and was just settling it on his head when Gretel came bursting in. "We're free!" she panted.

"Of course we're free," Hansel said, smoothing and fluffing the wig.

"No, no, no," Gretel explained impatiently. "We can escape now. I pushed the witch into her own oven."

"No!" Hansel cried, and he ran into the kitchen with great speed, because he knew the secret of running in high heels. But when he pulled the oven door open, there was absolutely nothing inside. "We've got to find her," he said. And while Gretel followed him uncertainly, he looked through every room of the cottage. But the lady was nowhere to be seen.

Finally he went back into the dressing room, and as he passed in front of the triple mirror he saw her. She had big bouffant hair, and the light broke and danced on her dress, and oh, she was beautiful. When Hansel smiled with joy to see her, she smiled back, and when he raised his hand to his face, the lady raised her hand in farewell. "Why, I'm a star," he said, and he was amazed. "It *is* time for me to leave." He put on a wrap of white fur and walked to the door.

"But what about me?" Gretel asked sadly.

Hansel looked at her. It's true she wasn't glamorous, but he thought how clever she must have been to trick the lady into the oven. So he said, "You can be my manager."

When the two of them opened the macadamia-nut-brittle front door, they found a path that ran all the way out of the Great Forest. Away at the end of it, tiny with distance but twinkling with many lights, they could see a city. Above the city searchlights swung this way and that, as if announcing the premier of a new star. And so, hand in hand, Hansel and Gretel set out together.

RUMPELSTILTSKIN

ONCE THERE WAS a young man named Steven, who when he turned eighteen, was brought by his parents to live with his uncle the miller. The miller had never married; Steven's parents had a feeling their son was never going to marry, either, and they hoped the miller might finish their son's education and show him how to get on in the world in ways they couldn't.

Well, the miller had always been fond of his nephew and was happy to take him under his wing. During the day Steven worked in the mill and got plenty of exercise hauling heavy bags of grain and flour. In the evenings the miller took him to coffeehouses and the theater and gallery openings, where Steven met the miller's friends. Everyone liked him, and it was a pleasant life.

Now, the miller was a good man, but he had one failing, and that was that he couldn't resist bragging. He'd brag about anything, and it didn't matter whether it was true or not. If someone behind him at the concert said their suit cost an arm and a leg, the miller would turn around in his seat and claim that the one he had on cost him two members of his family. Or if a man ahead of him in line at the market told him about his dog who fetched the morning paper, the miller would wait impatiently and

"Rumpelstiltzkin," AL; "Rumpelstiltskin," GB; "Who Built Reynir Church?," SFFT.

then describe the dog he owned, who wrote a gossip column and was a whiz at typesetting, besides. It was like a fever that came over him, and everyone who knew the miller just rolled their eyes and let him talk.

One day the miller was down at the mill, chatting with two old friends. The three of them were watching Steven clean the millstones. After a while, the first friend remarked, "I've got a nephew myself, and that boy can make a silk purse out of a sow's ear."

The second friend said, "That's nothing. I've got a nephew who can make a mountain out of a molehill."

The miller couldn't let this pass. "My nephew Steven," he declared, "can turn shit into gold."

Now, the king just happened to be passing the mill on his afternoon walk. He stuck his head in the doorway and said to the miller, "In that case, have your nephew come to the castle tonight at seven."

The miller bowed and said, "Yes, Your Majesty." His two friends bowed as well, but they grinned at the fix their friend had gotten himself into.

In his youth the king had been a ferocious warrior, and before he settled down he'd slain every giant, troll, and dragon in the kingdom. Now his son—who was known throughout the kingdom as the Angry Prince—was possessed of the same fiery spirit, but there were no more enemies to subdue. The king was beginning to worry that when it came time for him to pass the crown on to his son, the Angry Prince, with no other channel for his natural aggressions, would take them out on his subjects and be a real tyrant. Already he had heard murmurings against the prince up at the castle. "He really dumped on me this morning," the sergeant at arms complained to the yeoman of the guard. "The prince always hands everyone a ration of shit," the duke observed to the count. "He's such an asshole," a scullery boy bitched to a page. But when the king heard the miller say he had a nephew who could turn shit into gold, he thought he may have found the answer to his problem.

That night, at quarter to seven, the miller and Steven stood on the front step of the castle. "Uncle, what are we going to do?" Steven fretted. "You know I can't turn shit into gold. Or into anything, for that matter."

The miller patted Steven on the shoulder with great confidence. "There's not a thing to worry about," he said. "You're smart, and you're cute, and everyone likes you. You'll think of something." Then he rapped the big brass knocker and hurried off as quickly as he could.

A footman in livery answered the door, and Steven explained that he was to appear before the king. The footman let him in and brought him over to the majordomo, who straightened Steven's collar and escorted him to the chamberlain. The chamberlain gave Steven's hair a quick brushing and introduced him to the minister of protocol, who thought the shine on his shoes wasn't quite up to the occasion but there really wasn't time to do anything about it and they'd just have to hope for the best. Pages and men-at-arms and courtiers with nothing much to do after dinner drifted over as well, and when it was judged that the crowd around him was suitably large, Steven was escorted into the throne room and presented to the king.

"Everyone leave except Steven," the king commanded, clapping his hands, and everyone did. The king pushed his crown back, rubbed the red mark it left on his forehead, and smiled. "Steven," he said, "I've heard great things about you."

"Aren't rumors terrible things, Your Majesty?" Steven asked hopefully.

"Now don't be modest," the king said. "Let's take a little walk. I'd like to show you something." He stepped down off the throne, tucked his hand into the crook of Steven's elbow—"Do you work out?" he asked—and the two of them left the throne room. They climbed an enormous white staircase, walked down some corridors, and arrived in that part of the castle where the nobility had their sleeping quarters. At last they came to a suite of rooms with a gold crown over the door. Two servants stood on either side of the door, bowing and opening it for them, but as he passed between them, Steven couldn't help noticing that one had a bandaged nose and the other a black eye.

Inside, the room was a ruin. Furniture was smashed, it looked as if someone had punched several holes in the walls with his fist, and a love seat had been stuffed into the fireplace and halfway up the chimney. "My son's room," the king said sadly.

"Very nice," Steven said, as politely as he could.

"No, don't be tactful," the king said. "It was a nice room, but now it's, well, my boy, if you'll pardon my French, shit. There's not much sense replacing anything because he'll just do it again." He sighed and shook his head. "Do you like it here at the castle, Steven? If you could see your way clear to help us out with your special gift, we'd love to have you come live here with us. Maybe be my son's companion. He's a good-looking boy, and I think you'll like him, if he doesn't kill you. And unless you truly know how to turn shit into gold, I'm afraid that's just what will happen. But why am I taking up your time? You probably want to get right to work. Good luck, my boy, I have every faith in the world in you." He clapped Steven on the shoulder and went out, closing the door behind him.

"What am I going to do now?" Steven groaned, not expecting an answer, as he was alone in the room.

But suddenly there was a rustling in the overturned wastebasket, and a funny little man crawled out, stood up, and dusted himself off. His tiny biker's cap, his tiny boots, as well as his tiny motorcycle jacket, body harness, and chaps, were all made of black leather. He took off his tiny mirrored sunglasses and tucked them into his jacket. "Hello, Steven," said the little man. "Looks like you have a problem."

"I have to turn shit into gold," agreed the unhappy Steven, "and I don't know how."

"I do," claimed the little man. "And I can show you how to do it, too."

"Can you really?" asked Steven.

"Oh, absolutely. It's what I do. Show you how in five seconds, ten at the most. What'll you give me?"

"I don't really have anything," Steven confessed. "What would you want?"

"Your happiness."

"Excuse me?"

"All of it."

Steven began to think that perhaps the little man wasn't as friendly as he seemed. The little man saw him hesitate and quickly said, "No payment for an entire year. And no one's going to offer you better terms than that."

They didn't really sound like such great terms to Steven. But he reflected that if he didn't accept them, he'd lose all his happiness that very night, and his life, as well. Then too, a year was a long time, and anything could happen before the little man's payment was due. So they shook hands on it. Actually, the little man was only able to shake the tip of Steven's finger, but he had a remarkably strong grip.

"All right," Steven said, massaging his finger. "Show me how to turn this shit into gold."

"This stuff?" the little man asked, making a face. "No, all this will have to go into the dumpster out back. Now listen. When the Angry Prince comes in and finds you in his rooms, he's going to throw a fit, and he'll want to fight with you."

"Then I'll fight him," replied Steven, who kept in pretty good shape carrying bags of grain at the mill.

"No, no, no," cried the little man. "You're not listening. He's not the Angry Baron. He's not the Angry Count. He's not the Angry Telephone Repairman, for heaven's sake. He's the Angry *Prince*. The king's son. You can't oppose him."

"I see," Steven said, nodding. "So when he comes in, I won't fight him. I'll let him do all the fighting."

"No, no, no," shrieked the little man, who seemed to have a very low threshold for frustration. "That won't work either. If he starts fighting with you, he'll kill you. Remember, he's the king's son, and you're— what is it now—a miller's nephew?"

"Then what should I do?" shouted Steven, getting a little frustrated himself.

"Hey," warned the little man. "Don't ever raise your voice to me. What you do, Steven, is simple. You get him to spank you."

"Oh," said Steven. "Oh, right. Of course." The little man was right: it was simple. So simple that Steven wanted to kick himself for not having thought of it on his own before agreeing to the unpleasant bargain with the little man. But there wasn't any time for kicking. From the hall- way came the sound of an angry voice, followed by several slaps and punches. The little man winked at him, stamped his tiny boot, and dis- appeared. Then the door slammed open, and the Angry Prince stormed into the room.

"What are you doing in here?" he roared as soon as he saw Steven. He would have been a very handsome young man, but oh, he was knot- ted up with tension.

"I'm sorry," Steven said in his mildest voice. "I won't do it again."

This made the Angry Prince pause. Generally he found that people responded to his rages with the most irritating excuses or with rages of their own—even more irritating—and he was momentarily at a loss as to how he should proceed. He rallied himself. "Well, you shouldn't have done it in the first place," he shouted.

"You're right," Steven shouted back. "Why don't you spank me?"

"Really?" asked the Angry Prince. No one had ever made such a sug- gestion to him before, and he could feel some of the tension begin to leave his neck and shoulders.

Steven gave him his most charming smile, and that was very charm- ing, indeed. "Really," he said.

Meanwhile, the king waited out in the hall in a state of some apprehension, which wasn't lessened by the nature of the sounds coming from within his son's rooms. It seemed the Angry Prince was venting his rage on the miller's nephew, though oddly enough Steven wasn't crying for help. Well, sighed the king to himself, that's what happened to people who claimed they could turn shit into gold when they really couldn't. He had a servant bring him a comfortable chair and settled down to wait for whatever the morning brought.

It was almost noon when the door finally opened, and to the king's amazement his son and Steven walked out together, arm in arm. Steven looked radiant, and the Angry Prince could hardly be recognized, he was so relaxed—he actually smiled. The king peeked into the room. The broken furniture hadn't been turned into gold, and that was a little disappointing. But when he saw his son pass between the two doormen without striking either of them, he said to himself, Well, *something's* certainly changed. So Steven came to live at the castle in a suite of rooms that communicated with the Angry Prince's—who for the first time in his life began to be known by his given name, Eric. And for a year, Steven's life was delightful.

But one night, as he was doing his sit-ups, the wastebasket in the corner suddenly tipped over, and out crawled the little man. Steven had completely forgotten about him and wasn't happy to be reminded. "Hello, Steven," the little man said, dusting himself off. "Here I am for your happiness."

Well, Steven had gotten used to being happy. It seemed to him that though the little man had told him the secret of turning shit into gold, Steven had really done it himself. So he offered the little man jewels, or a position at court, or a lifetime membership in the gym of his choice, or anything else he wanted, instead. But nothing else would satisfy him. So at last Steven shook his head and said, "I'm sorry, but you're just going to have to go away empty-handed, because you can't have my happiness."

"Really," the little man remarked. "Guess what, Steven? You're HIV-positive. See you around."

"No!" Steven cried. But something inside him said, "Yes," and he knew that the little man had just taken away his happiness.

Steven begged and pleaded with the little man, who enjoyed that. When he'd enjoyed it enough, he said, "Well, Steven, I can't just give you back all your happiness; I'd love to, but that's not the way these things work. However, I could make you a special, one-time-only offer. If you can tell me, in these next three nights, three guesses per night, why you're positive, what that means about you as a person, I'll give you back enough happiness to live a good life, and we'll be quits. *But*, if you can't tell me, then I keep your happiness, and I take you as well. Make your mind up quickly, I'm very busy."

Steven wasn't happy with the offer—he wasn't happy with anything at the moment. But he had a chance to change that, so he held out his finger for the little man to shake.

"All right," he said, rubbing his finger. "I'm positive because . . . God thinks I'm a bad person? Sex equals death? Too many poppers?"

"I like those guesses," chuckled the little man. "I like them because they're wrong." Then he stamped his boot and disappeared.

The next night it was the same story. "A plague created by homophobic scientists?" Steven guessed, clutching at straws. "Chronic feelings of worthlessness having an impact on my immune system? Nature's way of telling me I'm not what she had in mind?"

The little man beamed at him. "Oh, you're doing just fine," he said, shaking his head. "Don't bother packing a suitcase tomorrow night, Steven. You won't need anything where I'm going to take you." He stamped his boot and disappeared.

Steven was getting desperate. He sent for the only person he could think of who might be able to help him: his uncle. When the miller showed up, a little grumpy because it was so late, Steven told him everything. "So you see, Uncle," he concluded, "if I don't find out what having the virus means about me, I'm lost. I need you to go throughout the kingdom, talking to everyone you meet. Someone's sure to know the answer."

"Nephew, there isn't a thing to worry about," the miller assured him. "I'll handle everything." He didn't wait for morning to come but set out from the castle immediately.

Steven waited all the next day, unable to eat, unable to concentrate on anything. Finally, long after dark, the miller stumbled back in. He threw himself down in a chair. "I'm bushed," he groaned. "I must have talked to every single person in the kingdom today. My feet are killing me."

"I'm sorry," Steven said, trying to be patient. "We'll get you some Epsom salts. But did you find an answer for me?"

"Well," the miller admitted. "No."

"No?" Steven cried. "No one could tell you anything? Anything at all?"

"Oh, everyone had an opinion," the miller told him, waving his hand as if brushing away flies. "This one thought it was a punishment from God, that one thought it meant you didn't love yourself enough—you wouldn't believe some of the things I heard. But no one knew." He shook his head in disgust. Then he brightened up. "But I saw the most interesting thing—maybe this will take your mind off your problems. As I was cutting through the forest just now, I saw a light up ahead of me. What could that be at this time of night? I asked myself. So I crept up to it, and what do you think? I found a huge bonfire, with a little man in leather dancing around it, singing away at the top of his lungs and just having a wonderful time. Now, how did his song go? Oh, yes—listen to this." And the miller leaned forward and sang,

> "Last night wrong and the night before,
> he's only got three guesses more.
> Tonight I take him, fair and square:
> it's just something that was there.

Amusing little song, isn't it?"

"Uncle, it's the answer!" Steven cried, hugging the miller. He had no sooner hidden him behind the drapes when the wastebasket fell over and out came the little man.

"We're going to have such fun tonight, Steven," he cried, his eyes twinkling merrily. "Oh, yes! So let's get your three wrong guesses over with fast, because you and I have a long way to go."

"Let's," said Steven in an agreeable manner. "Does being positive mean I'm loyal in my friendships, honest, and dedicated to personal growth?"

The little man stopped grinning. "Uh, no," he said.

"Well, then, does it mean I'm creative, exciting, glamorous and courageous?" Steven asked.

"What are you talking about?" the little man growled, his eyes narrowing. "It doesn't have anything to do with those things."

"In that case," Steven said, leaning down and straightening the little man's leather jacket, "it must not mean anything about me at all. It's just a virus I was exposed to. A terrible one, but just a virus." And he pinched the little man's cheek.

"What?" shrieked the little man, his face turning as black as his outfit. "What? You—what did you say? What did you say to me? After all I've done for you?" He glared at Steven as if he'd like to do, well, what he thought until just that moment he was going to get to do, and he stamped his boot. But it went right through the floor and stuck there. This made the little man so furious that he gripped it with both hands and yanked it with all his might. Unfortunately for him, he pulled so hard that he tore himself in two, and that was his end.

As for Steven, he got back more than enough happiness to live a good life with his prince. When the king found out the part the miller had played in all this, he was so impressed with him that he invited the miller to come and live at the castle. And that's where the four of them are now.

ROMAINE

THERE ONCE LIVED a woman, and the woman was going to have a child. So she thought the old room at the back of the house would make a good nursery, but it needed some cleaning up first. She swept out the cobwebs, and she mopped the floor, and she scrubbed the walls, but when she washed the window she stopped, because she found herself looking out on a garden she'd never seen before. Well, not a garden, exactly; more of a vacant lot full of old bottles, and milkweed, and a car up on cinder blocks where its wheels should have been. But in one corner someone had cleared away the weeds and planted romaine lettuce. Suddenly the woman thought how nice a salad would be for lunch; and then she thought there was nothing in the world she wanted more than a salad; and then she thought that if she didn't have a salad of fresh romaine lettuce, she'd die. So she took to her bed and prepared herself for death.

Her husband came home from work. "What's wrong, honey?" he asked, alarmed at her rapid deterioration.

"I'm dying for a salad of the romaine lettuce I saw growing in the garden behind the house," sighed the woman.

"Rapunzel," AL; "The Godchild of the Fairy in the Tower," BBFF; "The Garden Witch," IF; "Rapunzel," GB.

This confession did nothing to comfort the husband, who happened to know that the lettuces and the lot they grew in belonged to an ogre. "What about baby mixed greens?" he offered. "They're on special at the grocer's." But no, she wouldn't have baby mixed greens, she wouldn't have Belgian endive, she wouldn't have radicchio—it was the ogre's romaine or she was off to the next world. There was nothing for the husband to do but step out his front door, climb the chain-link fence, and bring the woman back a head of romaine lettuce. It had a wonderfully reviving effect on her.

Next day, the husband came home from work and found her in bed again. "What?" he cried.

"Salad," she sighed.

He thought he'd better lay in a supply for her and then maybe this unfortunate craving would pass, so over the chain-link fence he went with a shopping bag. He had it halfway filled when a shadow fell over him; he looked up, and there was the ogre, casting it.

"What are you doing?" asked the ogre.

"Nothing," said the husband.

"Yes, you are," said the ogre, frowning at him—not a pretty sight. "You're stealing my lettuce, and I've caught you. Here, see if you can guess what's going to happen next." He picked up a head of lettuce and squeezed it to a pulp.

"Mercy," cried the husband, which was like crying "Water!" in the desert: if there were water around for the asking, it wouldn't be a desert.

"Concussion," countered the ogre, getting a good grip on the husband's shirt and pulling back a giant fist. "Emergency room. Restorative surgery."

"They were just lettuces," protested the husband. "My wife had a craving—she's pregnant."

"Pregnant?" repeated the ogre. An idea began to come to him—a long journey. "All right, little man," he said at last. "You took something from me, so now I'll take something from you. The baby."

"Monster!" the husband gasped.

"Keep your shirt on," growled the ogre. "I don't want to eat it. I want to raise it to be an ogre, like me."

Well, the man argued and pleaded, but what chance did he have against an ogre? Very little. He took his shopping bag of lettuces back to his wife and told her of the abominable bargain. She consoled herself with salad.

When the baby was born—a boy—the ogre was there to take him. As he received his prize, he grinned and said, "His name will be—"

"Romaine," said the woman. So Romaine it was, though the ogre had been planning on Sluggo. He carried Romaine away, and neither the woman nor her husband saw him again.

The ogre took his ward to a hunting lodge he owned, deep in the forest, and began the boy's ogrish upbringing. But from the very first, Romaine proved resistant. No matter how he tried, the ogre couldn't teach the little boy to crush bunnies instead of hugging and petting them. "Like this," coaxed the ogre, showing how it was done. "This is how we ogres do it."

When he was old enough to talk, Romaine began to put forth his own views on the subject. "I don't think I'm an ogre," he said.

"Of course you are," scoffed the ogre. "You're an ogre same as me."

Romaine wasn't convinced. He never played with the toy trucks or guns the ogre got him for his birthday, preferring to make dolls out of bits of fabric or, when the ogre ate those, endless chains of wildflowers. During football season, when the ogre insisted the boy sit with him in front of the television for what seemed forever, Romaine would lose himself in daydreams. "Pay attention!" the ogre would snap. "Ogres love football. Which one's the quarterback?"

"I have no idea" was the boy's weary answer. "I don't think I'm an ogre."

"Yes, you are!"

Secretly, the ogre found the boy fascinating because he was so unlike everything the ogre knew. Because he wasn't given to self-reflection, the

ogre wasn't in on this secret. Still, it exerted its influence on him. So it
was that, even as he pressured Romaine to act like an ogre, he completely neglected to make him look like one. Instead of the standard
ogre's crewcut—traditionally done at the kitchen sink with a pocket
knife—the boy's hair was never cut at all. It grew throughout his child-
hood, throughout his adolescence, until by the time Romaine was a
young man his hair streamed and flowed and waved behind him like a
pennant in the slightest breeze.

But as Romaine's hair grew, so did the ogre's frustration and impa-
tience. One night he brought something home in a burlap sack and
dropped it on the kitchen table, where it kicked and struggled and yelled
with great energy. "This," declared the ogre over the noise, "is a traditional favorite of ogres. I went to a lot of trouble to get us one. Make stew
out of it." And he stomped into the den to watch the news.

When Romaine untied the sack, a boy wearing thick-lensed glasses
with a book of poetry under his arm popped out. "Don't eat me!" yelled
the boy.

"Don't be ridiculous," said Romaine. "Of course I'm not going to eat
you." He let the boy out the back door, made stew out of the burlap bag,
and called the ogre in to dinner.

The ogre searched in his bowl, but all he could find was burlap. "You
didn't give me any sissy-boy," he complained, and then his face brightened. "Don't tell me you ate him all yourself," he happily accused Romaine. "I knew this would do it. No ogre can resist sissy-boy!"

"No, I didn't eat him," replied Romaine. "I didn't even cook him. I let
him go."

It was the last straw. "You, young man," stormed the ogre, "are an
ogre, and until you're ready to start acting like one, you can just be
locked up in a tower without doors in the middle of the forest!" And
since he just happened to have such a tower—having acquired it along
with all his other properties before the market went sky-high—he took
Romaine there and locked him up in the top of it. Every morning from

then on, he went to check on Romaine to see if he were ready to start acting like an ogre. But Romaine never was.

Now, the tower had no door, and naturally there were no stairs and no elevator. When the ogre wanted to see him, he would stand at the foot of the tower and shout,

> "Hey, Romaine,
>   Romaine up there!
>   I want to come up—
>   throw down your hair."

Romaine would then wind his long wavy hair once or twice around a hook set in the top of the one window and throw it down in a black cascade. The ogre would climb up, hand over hand.

One morning, as the ogre made his way to the tower, a prince happened to catch sight of him. The prince, whose name was Sean, thought it might be amusing to follow the ogre quietly, see what such a stupid brute was up to, and maybe play a trick on him if the opportunity should present itself. Sean was twenty-three, very handsome, and totally serious about keeping himself amused. His father was the king; everything he smiled at smiled back at him, and the world was a beautiful place.

The ogre stopped at the foot of a tower; Sean stopped behind a tree, watching.

> "Hey, Romaine!
>   Romaine up there,"

bellowed the ogre. A good-looking boy appeared at the high window.

"Nice," Sean observed to himself. "But how do you get up there?" Next moment, masses of black silken hair poured down the side of the tower. Sean caught his breath—he loved long hair. The ogre climbed up, and then, not having much to say to his prisoner, he climbed down and tromped away through the forest.

Sean came out from his hiding place. Softly he called,

> "Romaine! Romaine,
> up in the air,
> the way to heaven
> is in your hair."

Which wasn't exactly the way the ogre had phrased it but must have been close enough. Down came Romaine's hair, and when Sean took it in his hands, lightning shivered through him. He was up the side of the tower in no time and through the window of Romaine's prison.

"You're not the ogre," Romaine observed.

"No kidding," laughed Sean. He spread his arms so Romaine could catch the full effect of his radiance. "But maybe I'll do anyway," he suggested.

Romaine melted. They pulled his hair up together. All that day they had great joy in each other's company. When evening came, Sean kissed Romaine good-bye, promising to return next morning when the sun rose.

He did, timing his arrival after the ogre's departure, and the morning after that, and the mornings that followed. These were days of heaven for Romaine; Sean liked them, too. The two spent hours in each other's arms, and Sean told him stories of his father's kingdom, how someday he'd take Romaine there and the two of them would be happy forever. Now, it's not that Sean didn't mean what he said, but he was of an age where it seemed plans would come true if you just talked about them enough; meanwhile, what was so bad with things just the way they were? Nothing, as far as Romaine could see, and the ground around the base of the tower where he was still a prisoner burst forth with dark green heads of romaine lettuce.

But one morning when the ogre squeezed through the window, Romaine was deep in a daydream about his lover. "Why does it always take you so long to climb up the tower?" he wondered aloud, without considering the consequences of what he was about to say. "Sean gets up here in no time at all."

"Who's Sean?" the ogre wanted to know.

"The prince who visits me," replied Romaine.

"Are you out of your mind?" demanded the ogre. "Ogres don't visit with princes, we squash them."

"Oh, I could never squash anyone who kissed me as well as Sean does," Romaine assured him.

The ogre was completely scandalized. "You let a prince kiss you?" he bellowed. "That's the most disgusting thing I've ever heard of in my life! You're no ogre!"

"Isn't that what I've always told you?" asked Romaine. "May I leave the tower now?"

"I wouldn't have you in any tower of mine, buster," growled the ogre. "There's just one thing I want to take care of first." Romaine's hair was still wound around the window hook. The ogre whipped out a pocketknife and gave the boy his first crew cut. He threw him across his shoulder, climbed down the tower and carried Romaine away to a distant land, where life was very unpleasant and no one was happy to see him. Then the ogre hurried back to the tower, in order to give Sean a special welcome.

He didn't have long to wait. Soon Sean called from the foot of the tower,

> "Romaine! Romaine,
> up in the air!"

Romaine's hair fell out the window. It felt odd and lifeless to Sean, but he thought, "I'll bring him some conditioner tomorrow," and up he climbed. When he swung himself through the window, there stood the ogre. "Hey, you're not Romaine," protested Sean.

"Sure I am," said the ogre. "Come on in. Here, let me give you a hand." He grabbed Sean by the front of his shirt and threw him against the wall. "My boy was going to be the worst ogre the world ever saw," growled the ogre, squeezing his fists together. "But you ruined him. Now I'm going to ruin you."

"Give it a try, ugly," cried Sean, who worked out regularly and had every confidence in himself. He threw a punch that caught the ogre on the jaw.

Unfortunately, ogres love violence, even when it's directed against themselves, and the only effect the blow had was to make the ogre stronger. "You hit like a lily," he jeered. "Like a sick lily," he added, slamming one of his big fists into Sean's shoulder.

Now, he happened to hit Sean just as he said, "Sick." Sean, having been raised his entire life as a prince, had never been spoken to in such a way before. The result was that to his complete surprise, he lost all the strength in that arm. The ogre was quick to notice and take advantage of the situation. "Sick!" he cried happily, wading into the dismayed prince. "Sick, sick, sick!" Sean fought on as long as he could, but when the ogre punched him in one eye, then the other, his vision went dark, and his nerve broke. Escaping the ogre's assault, he groped his way to the window and jumped out. Fortunately, he landed on the lettuces growing at the foot of the tower, or it would have been the end of him. He fled deep into the forest, where he was a long time healing.

Although he eventually recovered his strength and set out from the forest to search for Romaine, Sean's vision remained clouded from the ogre's blows. Wherever he looked, there was darkness—cruelty and treachery, the strong dining on the weak and in turn becoming lunch for the stronger—a world where only dogs who ate other dogs made it to the next day. Sean decided he'd be one of the dogs who made it. He grew hard; he grew bitter; he grew proud of being so and counted no one his friend.

But if he no longer saw like a prince, he still looked like one. He journeyed from village to village, and everywhere were men who thought

him the happily-ever-after of their story. They made their hearts immediately available. Sean had no great use for hearts but helped himself to
money, wristwatches, anything small that could be readily pawned, and
continued on his way. Gradually he forgot that the reason he had a way
to be on was to search for Romaine; if he ever asked himself why he was
always on the road, the answer would have been that the only way to
survive a world as dark as this one was to keep on the move. And so Sean
wandered.

Meanwhile, in the distant land, Romaine had found a means of support and lived a quiet life. Perhaps because he was a stranger, or because
he was different from them, or because—who knows?—the people
there had ogrish blood, they gave him the task of collecting their trash.
Every day, Romaine would drive a clattering old truck through the
streets of the villages. Children announced his arrival with screams of
"Trash man, trash man, everybody's ash can," and pelted the side of the
truck—and Romaine, too, until he learned to keep his head low—with
stones. Then the villagers would bring out everything they wanted to
get rid of and throw it all into the truck. Oh, terrible things that they'd
inherited broken from their parents and had never been able to fix, that
they kept hidden from their wives, that none of the neighbors suspected
they'd had in the back of a drawer behind the odd socks—into the back
of the truck it all went. Then each villager would shout, "Off to the
dump with you!" and go back inside, feeling strangely relieved. And off
to the dump Romaine drove, where he unloaded his truck and where he
had a tiny shack that was his home. The dump was located on the top of
a hill, and there was a tendency for many of the terrible things to roll
back down into the villagers' houses, so that everything just had to be
thrown out again next day. But that's what Romaine was for.

Every night, though, Romaine shut his door, drew the tattered cur-
tains, and lit a candle. Gazing into the flame, he summoned up Sean's
face and remembered that once he had been happy, loved by a prince. He

told himself that Sean was still somewhere in the world, that someday they would meet each other again, and that Sean would keep the promise he'd made in the ogre's tower. Then Romaine lost himself in long dreams of what the new life would be like, when Sean took him away from the dump to his father's kingdom. And so Romaine waited.

Because the world is round, it happened one day that Sean in his wanderings came to the edge of the dump where Romaine waited. Romaine, wrestling a spoiled wedding bed from the back of his truck, looked up and saw his beloved. Sean, his eyes still full of darkness, didn't recognize him. But he recognized the look on his face. "How's it going?" he said, giving Romaine a grin bright as gold and hard as steel.

Romaine felt himself unrecognized. Have I changed that much? he asked himself, believing the answer must be yes. "It's going," he answered sadly, dragging the bed over to a pile of rubbish.

"I need a place to spend the night," Sean announced, as if telling this cute but oddly unresponsive guy that he'd just won the lottery.

"Well," Romaine replied, dusting off his hands, "you could stay here, if you don't mind sleeping in a dump."

"Tough luck for me if I do," observed Sean, grim. "The whole world's a dump."

They went into the shack. Romaine shared his meal, which was only what Sean expected, and when it was time to sleep, he told Sean he could have his bed. "Right," agreed Sean, with a smile that said, You can have everything you want tonight that I feel like giving you. He went into the tiny bedroom, climbed into bed, and waited for Romaine to join him. He waited; and he waited; and he waited; and waiting, he fell asleep.

When he was snoring, Romaine entered and stood looking down at his poor friend, who was in such greater need of rescue than he was himself. But how can you rescue someone who believes the entire world is a dump, especially if he thinks you're just another piece of its rubbish?

Romaine, who knew something about rubbish, didn't see any way to accomplish this, Sean was lost. He was lost, and he was also right there. Romaine wept.

He wept silently but copiously. The tears rained down on Sean's face, waking him, and when he opened his eyes, more tears fell into them. Now, Romaine's tears were extremely salty, and they burned. Sean blinked, shook his head, then put his fists to his eyes and rubbed, trying to rid himself of the irritation. As he did, the darkness of his vision cleared, and though the room was pitch black, it was only the shadow the world casts, and he recognized Romaine standing over him. "Where have you been?" he cried, opening his arms. "I've been looking everywhere for you."

"Here," laughed Romaine, sinking into his friend's embrace. "I've always been right here."

In the morning, they closed the door of the shack behind them and walked out of the dump without giving it a glance. If they had, they would have seen that it had become a garden during the night, where endless heads of romaine lettuce rustled and wore the dew like diamonds in the rising sun. They journeyed together to the kingdom of Sean's father, where the old king welcomed them and noted that wherever his son had been all this time, it had made him tougher and more fit to rule. Which was fine with the old king, who'd had his doubts about his son's ability to handle a kingdom.

Years later, Romaine and Sean, now king, had some business that took them through a depressed part of the kingdom. They passed a seedy bar just as the ogre, who had been inside spending his last dollar on a beer and watching daytime television, stumbled out. When he saw them together, the ogre was overcome with rage. "You're sick!" he yelled, as they disappeared down the street, oblivious to his diagnosis. "Both of you!" But the ogre was very much failed in health, and the effort was too much for him. As the words left his mouth, a fit of coughing took his breath away and didn't return it; he fell where he stood, turning to stone as he did. And if the wind and the rain haven't worn him away yet, he's lying there still, furnishing a rest stop for the pigeons.

THE TWO TRAVELERS

A HAIRDRESSER, WHO had been removed from his chair in the salon where he had worked for many years, set out into the world to seek another position. He entered a forest. As he walked, he happened upon a personal weight trainer who was between clients. "Since we're traveling in the same direction," the hairdresser observed happily, "why don't we go together? With two, the way is only half as long."

The weight trainer wasn't pleased at the idea of keeping company with a hairdresser, of all people—what if someone he knew saw them together and thought they were friends? But the forest was large and the way lonely, so the weight trainer shrugged and said in his gruffest voice, "OK. But keep your hands to yourself."

The hairdresser shrugged back at him and said, "Well, dear, one certainly tries."

Soon they came to a place where a second path split off to the left, and each of them looked at the two ways they might go. The weight trainer noted that the main path forged on straight ahead, while the one to the left quickly wound from sight among the trees. Believing himself to be the leader by virtue of his superior size and no-nonsense attitude, he stated, "We'll stay on the straight path. It's sure to take us somewhere worth going to."

"The Good Apprentice and the Bad," AFT; "The Two Travelers," GB.

But the hairdresser, from years of working with hair weaves, perma-
nents, and cellophane wraps, knew that things often weren't what they
at first appeared to be. So he looked at the two paths more closely and
observed that while the straight path became green and mossy further
ahead, the one winding away to the left was worn clear and smooth from
use. "I'm sure it's quite a lovely walk that way, dear," he said, as tactfully
as possible. "But if we actually want to get somewhere, I think the path
to the left may be our best bet."

Well, the weight trainer wasn't about to take directions from the hairdresser, because who knew to what sort of unsavory place that might lead
him? So he scowled and said, "The straight path is the right path, and the
right path is the path for me." And off he marched to the right.

The hairdresser sighed and took the path to the left. In a while he
came to a village, where he took a room at an inn, ordered dinner, and
got a good night's sleep. Next morning, who should come trudging into
the village, footsore and muddy, but the weight trainer. His path had
ended in a swamp, where his heavy build had worked against him, and
after freeing himself from one boggy pool only to blunder into another,
he'd finally backtracked to the fork in the paths and taken the one on the
left. The sight of the hairdresser, seated comfortably in the village square
enjoying the morning sun, did nothing to increase the weight trainer's
fondness for him.

But the hairdresser was glad to see him and, insisting he come and
have breakfast at the inn, caught him up on all the village gossip while he
ate. "And what do you think?" the hairdresser asked breathlessly, as the
weight trainer finished his third bowl of oatmeal. "The king is looking
for a personal weight trainer and a hairdresser. Could anything possibly
be more you and me?"

It was decided between them that they would travel to the king's castle together, and as it was many days' journey away, each would buy and

carry his own provisions. The weight trainer loaded himself up with containers of Muscle Growth 5000 and protein drinks, carrots, wheat germ, and oat bran, bearing the enormous bundle on his back with ease. The hairdresser carried only a fresh baguette, a piece of brie, and a few grapes in a white paper bag. "That's not going to be enough," the weight trainer said disapprovingly.

"Oh, I'm a very light eater," the hairdresser assured him. "But I imagine we'll pass some cute little out-of-the-way bistro or patisserie. And if worse comes to worst—well, I doubt if you'll let me starve."

"I sure will," the weight trainer informed him.

"Oh, you," laughed the hairdresser, not believing him for a moment. "Always the tough guy." They set off into the forest.

Well, that day they both ate, but the following day the weight trainer dined alone. By the third day they still hadn't passed any bistros, and the hairdresser asked for one of the weight trainer's protein drinks. The weight trainer refused. "I have to keep my calorie intake constant," he said brusquely.

On the fourth day, the hairdresser again asked for a protein drink. "I do have to eat, dear," he explained, reasonably enough.

But the weight trainer, along with his pack of food, carried a grudge against the hairdresser for ignoring his sensible advice, for always being so cheerful, and for insisting on calling him "dear." So he said, "All right. You want a protein drink? I'll let you have one in exchange for one of your eyes."

"One of my eyes?" exclaimed the hairdresser. "You're not serious, are you?"

"Do I look serious?" replied the weight trainer, scowling.

The hairdresser had to admit that he did—in fact, he couldn't understand how he'd ever missed noticing how very serious the weight trainer looked. "A one-eyed hairdresser is not a happy thing," he observed. "But a dead hairdresser is even less happy." He gave the weight trainer one of his eyes and received a protein drink in exchange for it. The weight trainer put the eye in his pocket.

Next day, the hairdresser asked for one of the weight trainer's yogurt bars. The weight trainer noted sourly that even the loss of an eye hadn't dampened his traveling companion's mood. "Give me your other eye," he demanded, holding out his hand.

"A blind hairdresser?" sighed the hairdresser. "Well, maybe I can teach myself to give stylings by braille." He handed over his other eye, taking the yogurt bar in exchange. The weight trainer put the second eye away in his pocket with the first. Then he tied one end of a rope around the hairdresser's neck and, taking the other end in his hand, led him through the forest.

But if he'd thought that now, certainly, the hairdresser's spirits would be crushed, he was doomed to disappointment. Even when the hairdresser tripped and fell—which the weight trainer made sure happened as often as possible—he just said, "Whoopsie-daisy," and picked himself back up. Soon he'd learned to keep his balance.

"Why are you so cheerful?" the weight trainer finally demanded.

"I don't know," the hairdresser confessed. "Sometimes someone will come in with a really awful home permanent or totally thin hair and tell you to make them beautiful. You just have to be able to make the best of a bad situation."

"Really?" asked the weight trainer. He sat the hairdresser down beneath a dead tree, tied the rope around its trunk, and said, "See what you can do with this." Then he went on his way, glad at last to have gotten the better of his irritating companion.

The hairdresser happened to be sitting on a spot where trolls had once surprised and killed a man, as trolls will do if they're not kept down. Where the man's blood had been shed, an herb patch had sprouted, a low-growing plant something like clover, with tiny triangular pink flowers. As the hairdresser sat there in the herb patch, reflecting that if he hadn't been a little blind to begin with he wouldn't be where he was now, a pair of ravens flew down and perched on a branch of the tree. "Things look bad for him, don't they?" the first raven observed.

"Terrible," agreed the second. "Too bad there's not more meat on him."

"Too bad he doesn't know what he's sitting in," the first one said.

"And what's that?" asked the second.

"Those flowers," replied the first. "If he crushed them and rubbed the juice in his eye sockets, he'd get eyes back in no time."

Now, from years of listening to gossip while he cut hair, the hairdresser had acquired the ability to understand anything he heard if he paid attention. He picked some of the flowers, crushed them between his hands, and applied the juice to his empty sockets. He got new eyes immediately, sharper than his old ones had ever been. The ravens were so startled at having their conversation understood by a man that they took off out of the tree, crying, "How? How? How?" The hairdresser untied the rope from his neck and continued on his way.

After a while he came to a walnut tree, the nuts black and ripe and ready to be eaten. "Well, well. Walnuts," he marveled. "Just the thing for a hungry hairdresser." And he reached up to pick some.

Just then a squirrel, who had made her nest in the tree, scampered out along a branch. "What's that you're doing?" she demanded.

"Helping myself to a little something to eat, dear, thanks for asking," the hairdresser replied.

"Oh, don't, oh, don't, oh, don't," the squirrel chattered, and she got so nervous that she rubbed her small black hands over her head again and again.

"But why not?" the hairdresser asked.

"This is the only nut tree for miles and miles around," the squirrel told him. "My babies need these walnuts. If you take any, they'll starve.

Please don't starve my babies!" And she began to sob quite loudly for such a small creature.

"There, there, it's all right," the hairdresser reassured her, though for the life of him he couldn't imagine how a few baby squirrels could possibly need every walnut on such a large tree. "I'll find something else to eat." The squirrel thanked him profusely, and he continued on his way.

He walked on until he came to a pond, where a duck had made a nest for herself and was sitting on her white eggs. "Wonderful," the hairdresser said, and he shooed the duck off the nest.

"What did you have in mind?" the duck inquired nervously.

"I haven't been eating all that well lately," the hairdresser told her. "I thought I'd just borrow a few eggs and, well, you know."

The duck became very agitated. "Borrow?" she cried. "Borrow my babies? For what? For omelettes, that's what. For frittata. For quiche. Oh, please, sir, don't borrow my babies." She began crying so that the tears ran down her bill and rolled off her feathers.

"Good heavens, dear," the hairdresser hastened to comfort her. "I don't know what I was thinking. I'll find something else to eat."

"Bless you, sir," sobbed the duck. The hairdresser continued on his way.

Well, what with the lack of food and sleeping out in the open, the hairdresser began to sneeze. "Oh, fine," he fussed. "Now I've picked up a cold." Just then he came to an orange tree, the oranges on it so ripe they were almost red. "Here's just the thing," he said. "Some fresh orange juice will do me good." He reached up for an orange.

Suddenly a tiny voice said, "What's that you're doing?"

The hairdresser looked around but couldn't see anyone. "Who said that?" he asked.

"I did," the tiny voice said. "I'm a cold germ, and you know perfectly well fresh orange juice will kill me. Won't you please reconsider? A couple of days, three at the very most, and I'll be gone. I'm just passing through you."

"Good heavens," the hairdresser exclaimed in exasperation. "At this rate I'm not going to have anything to eat at all. But all right, we've all got to live. Do you mind if I blow my nose once in a while?"

"As often as you like," the germ said grandly. "And thank you for your consideration." The hairdresser sneezed twice and continued on his way.

At last he reached the king's castle. He told the porter why he was there and was shown to the royal salon. It was most handsomely appointed, the chair like a throne, the lighting excellent, and the supply of mousse and styling gel more bountiful than any the hairdresser had ever seen. The king entered and took his seat in the chair. "I need a new look," he said.

"Certainly," said the hairdresser, tucking a strip of tissue around the king's neck and carefully settling the drape over him. "What are we doing for you today?"

"I don't know," growled the king, looking at his reflection with deep dissatisfaction. He was a morose, heavy set man with a long beard and an unruly head of gray hair under his crown. "Use your imagination. If I like your work, you're hired. If I don't, you're beheaded."

"Job incentive," the hairdresser remarked brightly. "Let's start with a shampoo. Mind if we take this off?" He removed the king's crown, setting it aside, then turned the chair around and gently lowered it back until the king's head lay in the sink. "You have a beautiful head of hair to work with," he observed, massaging the king's scalp under the warm water.

Well, he gave the king a very becoming crew cut, trimmed his mustache so his mouth could see the light of day, and clipped his beard short enough to reveal the line of his jaw. While he worked, he kept the king

amused with a stream of discreet compliments and slightly catty anec-
dotes. When he finished, he brushed the king off and held up a mirror
for him. "There," he said appreciatively. "You're gorgeous."

"I am, aren't I?" the king agreed, taking the mirror to check the back
and sides. "I like your work. You're the new royal hairdresser." The hairdresser gave a sigh of relief and asked if he might have some breakfast. In
the days that followed, the king came by for a trim every morning, lin-
gering to gossip and discuss matters of grooming.

Now, it so happened that the weight trainer had reached the castle
first. He'd secured a position for himself by telling the king that as a king
was the biggest, most powerful man in the kingdom, it was obvious that
he should have the biggest, most powerful body. "Ruling a kingdom is
serious work," he'd said. "You need muscle to flex. You need bulk, with
zero percent body fat, so it's hard as granite. Like this." He'd flexed both
massive arms at once. The king had agreed that size and solidity were exactly what he had in mind, taking it for granted—in the way kings sometimes have—that in a week or so he would have arms even bigger than
the weight trainer's.

But as it turned out, the king didn't enjoy working out. The constant
repetitions annoyed him, the lack of immediate results made him impatient, and the first time the weight trainer tried pushing him, saying,
"No pain, no gain"—which, to be fair to him, was only part of his job—
the king stonily replied, "That's just what I tell the royal executioner."
The weight trainer backed off immediately. He became frustrated, fearful
for his position and for his life as well, if he couldn't deliver the results
he'd promised.

None of this was helped by the arrival of the hairdresser. The weight
trainer couldn't understand why he wasn't still in the forest, leftovers
from some animal's lunch. But when it became apparent that his rival
had supplanted him in the king's favor, he knew he had to crush him immediately. Not just for his own sake but for the king's as well, because

what sort of influence could a hairdresser exert on the man who ruled the kingdom? Not a good one.

He knew that the king was restless and unhappy about growing older. One day, as he was spotting him on the weight bench, the weight trainer remarked, "I hear that hairdresser of yours says he can restore lost dreams."

"Really?" grunted the king, signaling that he wished to be relieved of the barbell. "Have him sent to me."

When the hairdresser arrived, the king said, "My friend, what's this I hear about you being able to bring back lost dreams? Mine have been missing for a few months now. If you can find out where they've gone and return them to me, I'll be most grateful. But I'm warning you, if you can't, I'll be most unappreciative, and I'll have your head. Have them back for me by the end of the week."

That night the hairdresser sat alone in his room, groaning over the impossibility of his task. Suddenly there was a scratching and pattering along the ledge outside his window, and in climbed a young squirrel. It was one of the babies of the squirrel who had asked him not to take any nuts from the walnut tree. "What's the matter?" the squirrel asked.

"I have to find out where the king's dreams have gone," the hairdresser explained mournfully, "and return them to him in a week. I don't have the faintest idea how to go about it, and if I fail he'll have my head."

"Let me see what I can do," the squirrel said, and with a whisk of his tail he was gone.

Two nights later he was back. "I climbed in the king's bedroom window," he reported. "The king has a young boyfriend. Every night, after the king falls asleep, the boyfriend quietly gets out of bed, slips down the hallway, and meets his lover, the captain of the guard. The king tosses and turns until his boyfriend comes back just before dawn, and that's why he doesn't dream anymore." The hairdresser thanked him for the information.

The next day when the king's boyfriend showed up for his twelve-thirty appointment, the hairdresser leaned down and murmured in his ear, "Have you heard the latest? That cute captain of the guard's got himself a new sweetie. Everyone's dying to find out who it is. We're all going to get together tonight and keep a watch on his room—it'll be a watch party! Isn't it exciting?"

The king's boyfriend turned pale but didn't say anything. That night, and the next, and the next as well, he stayed in the king's bed. The king slept soundly and dreamed beautiful dreams. And as he was no longer meeting the captain of the guard, the king's boyfriend was much more attentive and affectionate, which greatly improved the king's outlook. At the end of the week the king called the hairdresser before him.

"I don't know how you did it," he confessed. "But my dreams are back better than ever." He rewarded the hairdresser handsomely, and this did nothing to endear the latter to the weight trainer, who determined to send more trouble the hairdresser's way the first chance he got.

The next day, while he held the king's feet for a set of sit-ups, the weight trainer said, "I hear that hairdresser of yours says he knows how to restore lost youth."

"Does he really?" the king panted, falling back with a thud. "That's enough for today. Have him sent to me." When the hairdresser arrived, the king said, sipping his sparkling water, "My friend, why do you keep these gifts to yourself? If you can restore lost youth, why not restore mine?"

That night the hairdresser sat lamenting in his room. "I could take a few years off of him with a new look," he said to himself. "I could touch up the gray for him—well, it'd take more than just a touch. I could give him a collagen facial. But how can I possibly restore his youth?"

Just then there was a flapping of wings at the window, and a healthy young duck lit on the sill. It was one of the ducks who had hatched from the eggs the hairdresser had spared. "What's the matter?" he asked.

When the hairdresser explained his dilemma, the duck said, "Let me see what I can do."

He flew down to the castle moat and dove under the water. Many years before, when the king was a little prince, his father had discovered him playing with a porcelain doll. The old king had indignantly taken her away from his son and thrown her into the moat. The duck located the doll down in the mud at the bottom and brought her up. "Give this to the king," he said, putting her into the hairdresser's hands.

The hairdresser cleaned the doll off, made her a new dress from his lace pillowcase, and fixed her hair. Next day he was shown in to the king. "Well," the king said expectantly. "Are you ready to restore my youth?"

"Of course," replied the hairdresser, hoping for the best, and he presented the king with the doll.

"Annabelle!" the king cried with delight. "Oh, Annabelle, where have you been? Look at your beautiful dress!" He spent the next several hours talking and playing with his doll, as happy as a child. When he remembered to, he rewarded the hairdresser handsomely. The weight trainer was furious.

"I've got to come up with something that this guy won't be able to do," he said to himself, and he pondered the matter as well as he was able. Now, he knew that the king very much wanted to build himself another castle, but with the way the economy was at present that just wasn't possible. And he knew that for all his cleverness, the hairdresser would never be able to lift heavy blocks of stone one on top of the other. "Because that's a job for a real man," he laughed exultantly.

So the next day, as he watched the king marching in place on the Stairmaster, the weight trainer said, "I hear that hairdresser of yours says he can build a castle just like this in a day." And seized by a sudden inspiration, he added, "From a single grain of sand."

"What an astonishing fellow," the king wheezed, leaning on the weight trainer's shoulder as he stepped off the Stairmaster. "This machine was installed in the wrong room. Obviously, it would be more effective in the dungeon. Remind me to have it moved. And have the hairdresser sent to me." The hairdresser was. "My dear friend, I've heard about your ability to make a castle, just like this one, from a single grain of sand," the king said. "Well, here's a grain of sand for you. Now, don't disappoint me."

That night the hairdresser sat in his room, the grain of sand on the table in front of him. "I suppose I'd better give myself a shave and a trim," he murmured sadly. "So my head will look nice when it's mounted on the castle walls."

Just then a tiny voice said, "What's the matter?" It was the cold germ. When the hairdresser told him of the impossible task, the germ said, "Let me see what I can do. I'll have to call in a few friends. I hope you don't mind, but it's going to be a little noisy." It was. All night long the hairdresser lay awake, listening to the sounds of tiny hammers and tiny drills and tiny voices shouting instructions to one another. In the morning, the germ called him over to the table, where the grain of sand lay just where it had the night before.

"Oh," the hairdresser sighed, greatly disappointed. "Well, thanks anyway for trying."

"Just give the grain of sand to the king," the germ assured him. "Tell him to look at it under a microscope."

The hairdresser was brought before the king. When the king saw the grain of sand, his eyebrows rose and then lowered like the lid of a coffin. The weight trainer smiled happily and flexed until he almost doubled in size. The hairdresser held up a hand. "If you'll just give this a look under a microscope," he suggested.

One was brought in. When the king peered at the grain of sand through the microscope, he was amazed to discover that it had been carved into an exact likeness of the castle. But even more astonishing, when he turned the magnification up as high as it would go, the king found that he could see into the window of the throne room, where a king just like himself was bent over a microscope. "Unbelievable," he said. "Tell me, if my microscope were stronger, would I find a grain of sand under his microscope that was carved in the likeness of a castle?"

The hairdresser lowered his eyes modestly. "I don't like to brag," he murmured.

Well, it wasn't at all what the king had in mind when he asked for a castle made from a single grain of sand, but he was delighted. "Clearly my hairdresser is a person of unusual accomplishments," he reasoned to himself. "The kingdom could only benefit from his influence." So he presented the hairdresser with a gold chain of office and made him Special Tonsorial Counselor and Adviser on Domestic Policy to the King.

The king also decided that what he really needed, rather than bulking up, was to make himself more flexible, and so he switched from weights to yoga. The weight trainer was dismissed. His resentment of the hairdresser consumed him. "I've been trying to do this the wrong way," he fumed to himself. He sat down under a tree a short distance from the castle entrance, determined to wait there until the hairdresser should venture out, at which time the weight trainer would simply snap him in two. As he waited, two ravens flew into the tree and perched on a branch. The first raven looked down at the weight trainer and said, "Now there's someone who's trouble for somebody."

"Somebody in trouble might mean lunch for us," observed the second raven.

"You said a mouthful," the first raven told him, and the two of them shared a dusty chuckle.

Just then the weight trainer glared up at the birds, wishing they would stop their croaking, as it was irritating to him. "Look," the first raven said indignantly. "Another one who understands what we're saying."

"Let's show him what we do to eavesdroppers," cried the second. They flew down and pecked out the weight trainer's eyes, then flapped away, cawing, "There! There! There!" The weight trainer, greatly distressed and confused, blundered off into the forest, where he banged from one tree to the next, until at last he remembered the eyes he had taken from the hairdresser in exchange for food. Removing them from his pocket, he brushed off the lint and set them into his own empty sockets.

It took him a moment to adjust to seeing the world in such a new way. But when he did, the first things that presented themselves to view were his own hands. They looked as large and powerful as they always had, but there was something funny about them. After examining them closely, he realized what it was: for all their size and strength, they'd been no use at all in prevailing over the hairdresser. He chuckled over this—the first laugh he'd ever had at himself; it lifted his spirits remarkably—and thought that rather than seeking out another position as a weight trainer, he just might look into a new career. Maybe physical therapy.

As for the hairdresser, he grew to be a person of great prominence in the kingdom, exerting a benign and stylish influence on everyone he encountered.

THE GOLDEN PARROT

THERE ONCE WAS a king, and in the very center of his castle grew a garden of sunflowers. This was the king's pride and delight. He loved to stride between the ranks of tall hairy stalks and gaze up at their fierce yet blank faces, so like the sun itself, so emblematic of a majesty he was pleased to compare to his own. But every so often, when the king stepped into his garden for a stroll before breakfast, he would find to his disgust that a rosebush had grown there during the night. Sometimes he was confronted by a rosebush blooming a deep and passionate red, sometimes a delicate pink, sometimes an insouciant yellow—it was all the same to the king. He wanted sunflowers and sunflowers only, and was he king or wasn't he? And since the answer to that could only be yes, he uprooted each rosebush with his bare hands as soon as he saw it, and burned it in a corner of the garden. It was no use calling his attention to the fact that the rose, for all its beauty, had thorns enough to put across its own point of view. The king would simply breathe through his mouth—since as everyone knew sweet fragrances made a man effete, effeteness made him effeminate, and effeminacy made him good for

"The Golden Bird" and "The Three Princesses in the Mountain-in-the-Blue," NFT; "The Bird of the Golden Feather," AFT; "The Golden Bird," GB; "The Golden Mermaid," AL; "The Golden Feather," EV; "The Bird in the Golden Cage," GFT; "Prince Hassan Pasha," "The Bird Flower Triller," and "The Bird Wehmus," IndF.

nothing—pull up the rosebush, and go back into the castle for Band-Aids.

As the years went by, the king found a rosebush in his garden more and more frequently, until at last it was a daily occurrence. Now, the king was growing old, as even the best kings will, and he wasn't really one of the best. He began to be haunted by the fear that after he was gone—which would be many, many years from now and might after all never happen but it was best to be prepared, that's what separates the truly magnificent kings from the merely competent—after he was gone, a rosebush might get a foothold in his splendid garden, and then another, and then more yet, so that eventually there would be no sunflowers growing there at all. The idea of all those colored blossoms gently rioting in the breeze, of that sweet fragrance wafting out from the castle into the country around, made him grind his teeth. And so he called his oldest son, Ron, to him.

"Boy," he declared, "something has to be done about this rosebush problem. I want you to keep watch in the garden tonight. Maybe a florist is sneaking into the castle."

"You can count on me, sir," swore Ron fiercely, always terrified of failing one of his father's commands. "I'll have that florist for you by morning."

"Good boy," growled the king. "This is why a man has sons." That night Ron settled himself down in the garden to watch for the intruder. But what is there to do in a garden of sunflowers at night? After a while Ron's eyelids grew so heavy, he thought he'd just put them down for a moment. In the morning, the king woke him with a kick to indicate how well pleased he was and pointed out the rosebush growing next to Ron's head.

The king called his second son, Don, and explained the gravity of the situation to him. Don, eager to pick up the king's favor that his older brother had finally dropped, said, "Leave it to me, sir. Whether it's a florist or an entire conspiracy of landscape designers, you'll have security restored in the garden by morning."

"Make me proud, boy," commanded the king.

That night Don took up his post in the garden and thought about what he'd do to the intruder when he caught him. This kept him alert for a while, but when that while was over there wasn't much to see in the dark garden. In fact, there wasn't any discernible difference between how the garden looked with his eyes open and how it looked with them closed. In the morning the king woke Don with a rap of his scepter and pulled up the rosebush that bloomed next to him.

Now, the king had a third son, whose name was Jamie, and the king had never been particularly fond of him. Jamie was different from his brothers, being neither ambitious, arrogant, nor aggressive. "You don't take after anyone on my side of the family," the king told him whenever he chanced to cross paths with Jamie in the castle, and that was about the sum of what he wanted to say to his third son. Unlike his brothers, Jamie wasn't obliged to hunt, or ride, or physically abuse the servants, or do any of the things the king believed fitted a prince to exercise authority over others later in life. Nor for that matter, was he encouraged to take his meals at the table or even make his presence known when there was company. He was treated like a guest who had far overstayed his welcome, and he had no companion except a little white chicken named Dorothy, but she was a great consolation to him. He carried her with him everywhere, talking to her, watching her scratch and peck for worms, and in general tending to her needs.

"I don't see why the roses bother you so much, Father," said Jamie. "But if you like, I'll sit in the garden tonight and see what I can see."

"Don't be ridiculous," the king said coldly. "Are you more of a man than your brothers?" And since he felt certain that the answer to this was no, he believed the matter had come to an end.

But Jamie, used to living with the king's neglect, had also grown accustomed to making his own decisions. That night he slipped into his father's garden, never one of his favorite places. But with the setting of the sun the sunflowers let their heads droop so that they looked graceful and almost demure, and Jamie thought perhaps they weren't all that bad. He amused himself counting glowworms and falling stars. So it was that when, just before dawn, a golden parrot with a diamond beak flew into the garden, perched on the tallest sunflower, and began cracking its seeds, Jamie was awake to see it. "Hello," he said, delighted.

"Hello, pretty," replied the parrot, and made a dropping.

Jamie, who knew something about the ways of birds from spending his time with Dorothy, held his hand up to the parrot, clucking in his most soothing manner. The parrot flew down to his hand. Just then the sun rose. Inside the castle, the king banged open his bedroom door and bellowed, "Rise and shine, everybody, it's a new day!" This was how he started each day; he was a morning person. The parrot immediately took wing, and though Jamie tried to catch it, he only succeeded in pulling a single golden feather from its tail before the bird disappeared into the sky. But when Jamie looked down, he saw that just where the parrot had made its dropping, a rosebush bloomed. Knowing his father would uproot the bush as soon as he discovered it, Jamie plucked a single rose and hid it in his shirt.

When the king stepped into his garden he looked at Jamie, then at the rosebush. It was hard to tell which sight displeased him more. He tore the bush out of the ground, and as he carried it to the back corner, Jamie told him where the roses came from. He showed his father the gold feather. "A golden parrot," the king said, taking the feather from him and turning it slowly in his hands. "How splendid a golden parrot would look in a golden cage—with a good heavy layer of newspaper in the bottom to catch all the droppings—in my garden of sunflowers."

He dismissed Jamie, who hurried away to enjoy the rose he'd saved. But when he took it out of his shirt, he found to his disappointment that the heat of his body had withered it, and the rose now smelled like he did—not a bad smell, by any means, but not the heavenly fragrance he'd looked forward to.

Just then Dorothy happened to pass by. When she saw the rose, she grew very excited and began clucking in a most agitated manner. "You want the rose, Dorothy?" Jamie asked, a bit surprised, since what she generally wanted were mealworms. "Well, here. You might as well have it." Dorothy didn't need to be offered it twice. She took the rose from Jamie's hand, tossed her head back, and gulped it down.

Meanwhile, the king called his two older sons into the garden, displayed the feather to them, and declared, "I will give half of my kingdom to whoever brings me the golden parrot." Well, Ron and Don each wanted the entire kingdom for himself, but they thought getting it would be simple for anyone who already possessed half of it. They volunteered to leave immediately. "May the best man win," pronounced the king, which was his way of giving them his blessing.

As they marched out of the castle, Ron and Don happened to pass Dorothy, pecking up a bit of gravel to aid her digestion. She looked up at them and remarked, "When you get to the village, spend the night in the dark inn, not the bright one." Ron and Don, far from being flabbergasted, let alone grateful for the tip, were highly indignant.

"Is this any sort of creature to be addressing two princes?" Ron demanded angrily.

"I don't take advice from chickens," Don asserted. "I eat them." And he tried to give Dorothy a good kick. But you know how hard it is to kick a chicken, and his effort came to nothing.

The brothers proceeded to the edge of their father's kingdom and entered the great forest. They walked all day long, and when night came, they found themselves in a village that boasted two inns, one on each side of the road. The inn on the left was small, dark, and shabby, not at all the sort of place where two princes with high self-esteem would care to spend the night. The inn on the right was another matter entirely. Its neon sign flashed confidently, music blasted out into the road, and the smell of rich greasy food accompanied it. It seemed far more appropriate to their station in life, and in they went. Over cocktails they made the acquaintance of two very convivial young women, and, after a heavy dinner followed by more cocktails, married them, raised up large families, and forgot all about the golden parrot.

Meanwhile, the king kept his garden lit with floodlights and staffed with net-wielding servants every night, in hopes he might save himself half a kingdom. The golden parrot stayed away, and though this kept the garden rose free, the king was dissatisfied and restless, preoccupied with the idea of possessing the bird. At last Jamie approached him. "Father," he said. "No doubt Ron and Don are doing their best. But with three searching, there's that much more of a chance the golden parrot will be found. Why don't I go out and look for it, too?"

"You?" repeated the king, the way a man might say, "Termites?" if told his house were infested with them. "Are you more of a man than my two sons? When I want advice about chickens, I'll send for you." And he believed the matter had been seen to its end. But Jamie, who'd never received any encouragement from his father, had long since ceased to accept any discouragement from him. He made himself some sandwiches for the road and went out to search on his own.

Leaving the castle, he passed Dorothy, who had just caught herself a large and rather frisky beetle. "Good-bye, Dorothy," he said. "I'm off to find the golden parrot for my father."

Dorothy looked up at him, allowing the beetle to beat a retreat for itself. "When you get to the village, spend the night in the dark inn, not the bright one," she advised.

"Dorothy!" Jamie exclaimed. "I didn't know you could speak."

"You're the light of my life, Jamie," Dorothy told him in her surprisingly deep voice. "But sometimes I wish I had a mealworm for everything you don't know, even about your faithful white chicken."

It occurred to Jamie that if you were going out to look for a golden parrot with a diamond beak, you could do worse than have a faithful talking chicken along for company. He put the matter to her. Dorothy was more than happy to be asked. "In fact," she said, "I know where you can find that parrot. He belongs to the king of the Castle After This."

"You're just a gold mine of information," Jamie said happily. "I don't know how I'll ever be able to thank you."

"When the time comes," Dorothy assured him, "I'll ask for something."

"Anything," Jamie promised. They set out together, comparing observations on life in the castle, which neither of them found completely satisfactory. Soon they came to the forest at the edge of the kingdom and entered it.

Night was falling as they reached the village of the two inns. Jamie didn't pay attention to the one full of light and laughter but went directly to the small dark inn and asked for a room for himself and his chicken. The innkeeper was delighted to have guests and gave Jamie the best room in the house, which in spite of the inn's appearance proved to be quite comfortable. Jamie passed a restful night, and in the morning the innkeeper brought them up a lovely Continental breakfast. They ate, and when they had put a bend or two of the road between themselves and the village, Dorothy said to Jamie, "Walking like this will take far too long. Step up onto my back, and we'll go fast." Jamie wasn't sure how fast even a chicken like Dorothy could go with somebody standing on her, but he did as she suggested.

Well, Dorothy went very fast indeed. The forest leapt by in a green blur, and when it stopped Jamie found himself facing a castle with a hundred armed guards sleeping on the ground before it. "That is the Castle After This," Dorothy said. "Walk past the guards boldly and they won't wake up. Climb up the stairs, and open the first door on the left. If you hold out your hand with confidence, the golden parrot will step right onto it and let you carry him out of the castle. But don't touch anything else you see in the room." Jamie agreed to do just as she said, and strode past the sleeping guards.

When he opened the door at the top of the stairs, he found a room filled with golden birds on perches. There were macaws and cockatoos and toucans, all silent, all watching him with bright eyes as he entered. Jamie walked up to the golden parrot with the diamond beak, held his hand out to it, and the parrot gave him its foot and stepped on. But as he was about to leave, Jamie reasoned to himself, "The parrot is for my father. But if I take a bird for myself, I can get rosebushes from its droppings. I'll just take one of the small ones." He reached for a lovebird. The moment he did, every bird in the room began to shriek, growl, twitter, and cry, and the golden parrot led them all. "Thief, thief, thief in the castle!" it screamed. "Hello, pretty!" In an instant, the room was full of guards, who surrounded Jamie and took him before the king.

"I can't tell you how much I dislike people who take what isn't theirs," the king said in a voice like cold split-pea soup. "Especially when it's mine. In order to wean you from this unsavory practice, I'm going to have your head taken off your shoulders." Then he seemed to give the matter further thought and said, "Unless, of course, you bring me the golden hunting poodle that outruns its own shadow. It belongs to the king of the Castle After That, but he wastes the dog's potential. I'm told he plays the occasional game of fetch-the-stick with it and the rest of the time allows it to lie in the sun. Whereas if such a magnificent creature were mine, I'd soon put it to work siring the finest breed of hunting poodles the world has ever seen. So, my young thief, you bring me the golden poodle, and I'll not only spare your life but give you my golden parrot as well."

Well, what could Jamie do? In order to retain his head, he agreed to bring back the poodle. Dorothy was waiting for him outside. She was very peeved with him. "Jamie," she scolded. "Most people would be content with a talking chicken and a golden parrot. I really should leave you here." But Jamie reminded her of all the times he had petted her and groomed her and brought her mealworms. At last she relented and said, "Well, we have to get to the Castle After That. Step up onto my back, and we'll go fast." So Jamie did, and they did.

When they stopped, Jamie found himself before a castle. A thousand armed guards lay sleeping in front of the gate. "This is the Castle After That," Dorothy told him. "Walk boldly past the guards, Jamie. Climb up the stairs and open the second door on the left. Approach the dog with confidence and he'll follow you. But under no circumstances attempt to put a leash on him." Jamie agreed to do exactly as she said this time, and he strode past the guards.

Behind the second door at the top of the stairs, he found himself face to face with a golden poodle the size of a lion—a large lion, at that. It sat on its haunches and watched him gravely as he entered. "Hello, boy," Jamie said, stepping up to it. He held the palm of his hand to its muzzle and then rubbed the magnificent crest of curls on its head. The poodle accepted this attention in a dignified manner. "Come on, boy, let's go," he said, turning to leave, and the poodle rose to its feet and allowed him to lead the way. Just then, Jamie saw a dog collar set with diamonds hanging on the wall beside a silver leash. "Such a splendid animal deserves a splendid collar and leash," he said to himself, and it certainly sounded reasonable. The poodle stared at him, completely affronted, as Jamie fastened the collar around its neck, but when he attempted to attach the leash it threw back its head and bayed. Instantly the room was full of guards, who surrounded Jamie and took him before the king.

"Dognapping is a capital offense," the king growled, glaring at Jamie as if he meant to leap on him and carry out the sentence personally. "As well it should be. There is nothing lower on this earth than a dognapper. Why, a person who would dognap would do anything—*anything*." He cast about for an example of what else a dognapper might stoop to, and came up with a perfect one. "For instance, a dognapper, if he knew what was good for him, would even journey to the Last Castle of All, kidnap the prince who's so handsome stars fall at his feet hoping he'll pick them up, and bring him back here so I can wed him to my daughter, the Princess Who Doesn't Seem to Want to Marry Anyone. This, of course, would enable me to spend my old age surrounded by grandchildren as handsome as their father and as selective as their mother. Naturally, I would respond with kingly generosity, rewarding said dog- and prince napper not just with his life but with my golden hunting poodle as well. Sound interesting?"

It sounded much more interesting than being executed, and Jamie agreed to bring back the prince for the king's daughter. He was let go. Outside he found Dorothy, so upset she wouldn't even speak to him. So he petted her and stroked her, and at last she relented and said, "I feel sorry for you because you seem so determined to do everything the hard way. Step onto my back, Jamie, and we'll go fast." So Jamie did, and they did.

When they came to a stop, Jamie found himself before yet another castle. A hundred thousand armed guards lay asleep in front of the gate, and the sound of their snoring made the earth tremble. "This is the Last Castle of All," Dorothy shouted. "I think you know how to proceed by this time. The prince is behind the third door to the left. If you kiss him before speaking to him, he'll follow you out of the castle. But under no circumstances—and please pay attention here, Jamie, because this seems to be the part that gives you so much trouble—under no circumstances allow the prince to take anything with him. Do you understand?" Jamie said he did, and swore that this time without fail he would do just as she said. He made his way to the third door and opened it.

Inside he found the prince, and Jamie couldn't have helped kissing him if the world depended on it, the prince was that handsome. So he did, for quite some while, then whispered, "Let's go."

"I just want to pack a few things in an overnight bag," the prince, whose name was Ellery, murmured back. Well, Jamie said no, but Ellery said please, and there might have been a man somewhere in the world who could have withstood Ellery saying please, but it wasn't Jamie. Ellery unzipped his overnight bag, and at the sound of the zipper unzipping the room filled with guards. They surrounded Jamie and took him before the king.

"Oh, it's an adventurer," observed the king, as if it were a species of butterfly too common to bother collecting. "Well, I suppose Ellery is old enough to go off with whomever he pleases. But since you're such an ambitious young man, I wonder if you could do me a small favor before you leave. Out behind the castle is a mountain I've grown rather tired of. I'd like you to take it away and replace it with a lake. As soon as you've done that for me, you can be on your way." Jamie was taken out behind the castle.

He labored with a shovel for three days, but the task wasn't as easy as it sounded. For one thing, it was rather a large mountain, covered with trees and crowned with ice and snow. For another, there was the problem of where to move it to: every shovelful he dug up had to be carried far off into the forest so it wouldn't get in his way later. It seemed he'd be at his labor for a hundred years, but on the evening of the third day Dorothy appeared. "Let me see your hands, Jamie," she said. He did, and when she saw that they were covered with blisters she nodded her head. "Very good," she said. "Go and get some rest." Jamie was happy to do so, and he stretched out under a tree and fell asleep.

Dorothy jumped to the top of the mountain and set to work. She began to peck and scratch, scratch and peck, and soon the mountain was gone. She scratched and pecked, pecked and scratched, and soon a deep valley lay where the mountain had stood. She pecked once more, gave a last scratch, and water began to well up in the bottom of the valley. By

morning a vast lake spread out behind the castle, reflecting the clouds
and the sun on its journey. The king was very pleased when he saw it.
"That's much better," he said approvingly. "We've needed a lake around
here for quite some time. Ellery, you've found yourself a young man of
real accomplishment. Good luck to both of you." The king kissed his
son good-bye, and Jamie, Ellery, and Dorothy went on their way back to
the Castle After That.

But by the time they arrived, Ellery had other ideas about how things
should go. "Forget it," he said flatly. "I'm not about to marry a princess.
It's me and you from now on, Jamie." This was fine and more than fine
with Jamie, but he was at a loss as to how he would acquire the golden
hunting poodle.

"Well, we'll just have to give the king something that looks like
Ellery, won't we," said Dorothy. She nestled down, gave a sudden cackle,
and laid an egg. "Break that, Jamie," she instructed.

He did, and there to his amazement stood a twin to Ellery. "How many
times do you think you could do that, Dorothy?" he asked innocently.

Ellery took him by the back of the collar. "Just once," he stated.
"Now go trade him for the poodle, he makes me nervous." So Jamie
brought the false Ellery into the Castle After That and presented him to
the king.

"Oh, you rascal," the king chuckled delightedly. "You scoundrel.
He'll make first-rate breeding material." He handed the golden hunting
poodle over to Jamie, who thanked him and left immediately. The king
put his arm around the false Ellery's shoulders and, taking him for a
walk through the castle, rhapsodized over the beauty of his daughter and
the joys of fatherhood.

He hadn't been going on for more than a few minutes when the false
Ellery turned to him and said, "You know, you've kept yourself in *really*
good shape for an older man." Then he reached down and gave the
king's bottom an appreciative pinch.

"Guards!" cried the astonished king. But before any guards could arrive, the false Ellery gave the king a particularly eloquent raspberry and melted back into a raw egg.

Jamie and his companions made their way back to the Castle After This. But as they neared it, the golden hunting poodle sat down in the road and refused to continue. As he was the size of a lion, and a large lion at that, no amount of pushing or pulling could make him budge. "I don't think you want to leave me, do you, boy?" said Jamie. The dog affirmed that this was so, thumping its pom-pommed tail in the road till the dust rose.

So Dorothy laid another egg, and when Jamie broke it, there stood a golden hunting poodle exactly like his own. He led the false poodle into the Castle After This and presented it to the king.

"What a magnificent brute!" laughed the king. "What a studly animal! Oh, yes, he'll sire me the finest breed of hunting dog the world has ever seen. You may take the golden parrot." So Jamie did and continued on his way. The king was eager to set the hunting poodle to stud as soon as possible, and led it out to the kennels behind the castle. On the way, the dog suddenly felt the need to urinate. But to the king's chagrin, instead of lifting a magnificent golden leg, the false poodle squatted down in a demure fashion to relieve itself. When it finished, it looked back over its shoulder at the king and gave him a very sarcastic dog grin. Then it dissolved into a raw egg.

"Well, Jamie," Dorothy remarked as they all walked along together. "You've won the prince, the golden hunting poodle, and the golden parrot, and now you're on your way home to claim half of your father's kingdom. So if you don't mind, I'd like to ask a favor of you."

"Anything, Dorothy," replied Jamie. "Just name it."

"I hoped you'd say that," said Dorothy. "It would be very helpful to me if you'd cut off my head and pluck out all my feathers."

"I can't do that," Jamie protested, horrified by the very idea.

"It's the only thing you can do for me," said Dorothy sadly. "And if you won't, I'll have to leave. But before I go, I have two pieces of advice for you. Don't have a family, and if you do, drink bottled water."

"Please stay, Dorothy," Jamie begged, but she didn't. He was grieved to lose his chicken and baffled over her two pieces of advice, which no matter how he turned them, didn't seem to fit anything. "It's not a matter of my not having a family, but of my family not having me. And what has bottled water got to do with anything?" But Ellery was a great consolation to him, and so were the poodle and the parrot.

The four of them walked on, and at last they reached the village of the two inns. They passed by a stucco duplex, with a tiny dirt yard full of screaming children. The two front doors of the duplex banged open, and out came two middle-aged men with enormous beer bellies, who cursed the children and kicked tricycles out of their way. When they saw Jamie, the two men's jaws dropped in astonishment. "Jamie!" they cried. "It's us, your brothers Ron and Don. We're on our way to the Brightly Lit Inn for a drink. Join us!"

"I really can't," said Jamie, not all that happy to see them. "I'm on my way home with the golden parrot."

"Home," said Ron, suddenly remembering that he was the son of a king.

"The golden parrot," said Don, suddenly remembering that he had once been on a quest for it himself.

"Oh, take us with you to see Father again," they begged Jamie. "Don't just leave us here—we're your family."

"Here's trouble! Careful! Careful! Hello, pretty!" said the golden parrot.

"Well," said Jamie doubtfully.

"Good, it's settled," cried Ron and Don, falling in line behind Jamie, Ellery, the parrot, and the poodle. They left the village behind and reentered the forest.

As Ron and Don followed along, Ron said to Don, "Looks good, doesn't he?"

"Well, why shouldn't he?" Don asked, tugging his T-shirt down over his big belly. "He's had it easy enough—roaming all over the world having fun while we've been raising families."

"He'll have it even easier, when he brings that golden parrot to Father and gets half the kingdom for it," observed Ron.

"That's not right," Don grumbled. "He's a single guy with no responsibilities. We've got *families*. We *deserve* the half kingdom."

Just then they happened to pass a well. Ron nudged Don. "Say, Jamie," he said. "You thirsty? This well has the best water you've ever tasted. Let's stop a minute."

"Not really," said Jamie, pausing to look back at his brothers. The golden hunting poodle and Ellery, with the golden parrot perched on his shoulder, continued walking.

"Oh, but you really should try some of this water," Ron insisted. "This is called the 'Well of Family Affection.' "

"Is it?" asked Jamie, walking over to look down into the well, which had a spiderweb spun across its mouth.

"It is for a fact, little brother," affirmed Ron. "The only problem is, there's no rope, so someone will have to be lowered into the well to bring up the water."

"Right," said Don. "And since we're much too powerfully built to fit, we'll lower you down. What do you say?"

"All right," Jamie agreed good-naturedly. "Only, let's hurry." So he let his brothers put him down in the well. When he reached the bottom and found it dry, he called up, "There's no water down here."

"Not for you there isn't," Ron shouted down. "You weirdo!"

He and Don hurried to catch up with Ellery and the golden animals, who in fact had started back to see what was keeping Jamie. "Jamie's going to catch up with us later," said Don. "He said for us to keep walking."

"I'll just go back and meet him," replied Ellery coolly, because he hadn't taken an immediate liking to either of Jamie's brothers.

"Uh, he's planning a surprise for you," Ron said. The golden hunting poodle gave a low growl, suggesting that this wasn't very convincing. "No, really," Ron insisted. "It's, um, it's something *special* he's got cooked up."

"That's right," Don concurred. "A special surprise."

"Likely story," squawked the parrot. "Hello, pretty."

"Hey, put a cork in it, Polly," snapped Ron, lunging for the bird. The parrot bit his finger with its diamond beak—with which it could exert considerable pressure—and took off in a blaze of golden feathers. Ron, cursing, ran after the parrot, Don sped after Ron, the golden hunting poodle raced barking after Don, and Ellery chased them all. As luck would have it, they were all at the very edge of the forest where it bordered the king's lands. Now, whether it was the forest that was enchanted or the kingdom, a sudden change occurred. As the golden parrot flew out from under the trees, it shrank into a common green parakeet that Ron easily caught. The golden hunting poodle, just about to seize Don by the scruff of the neck and give him a good shaking, was changed into an apricot teacup poodle with mange, who could do nothing more than yap and snap at the cuff of Don's pants. Ellery came pounding out of the forest, shouting, "What have you done with—" but as he set foot in the kingdom he instantly became an alcoholic waiter with skin problems. Since he was subject to blackouts, he couldn't remember what he'd just been doing, and his question remained unfinished.

When Ron and Don reached the castle, they found the king in his garden of sunflowers. "Father," they said triumphantly, "we've brought you the golden parrot."

The king was strangely unimpressed. "That's not a parrot," he stated, watching with distaste as the bird plucked out one of its feathers and began to chew it.

"Well, it's a very small parrot," said Ron optimistically.

"It's not golden," the king declared with a scowl.

"No, not in this light," admitted Don. "Could we have that half of the kingdom now?" But the king, never patient with failure, booted them out of the castle. The brothers took the parakeet away with them, wondering what to do next.

Meanwhile, down in the dry well, Jamie finally understood Dorothy's two pieces of advice. "Fine," he said. "Now what?" He tried waiting for Dorothy, but she didn't show up. "All right," Jamie counseled himself. "If she were here, what would she do? She'd probably try to go fast." So he tried to run out of the well, but it was too narrow and steep for that. "All right, then she'd lay an egg." But of course Jamie couldn't do that, so it was pointless even to bring it up. "Then the only other thing she'd be able to do would be to scratch and peck." And since Jamie had watched Dorothy do that more times than he could count, he had a fairly good idea how it was done. So he scratched, and he pecked. Nothing happened. He scratched and he pecked a second time. Nothing continued to happen. He scratched and he pecked a third time, and he uncovered a spring in the bottom of the well. The water bubbled up, and as its level rose, so did Jamie, until at last he was able to climb out and onto the forest floor again. Dorothy was waiting for him. "Dorothy," he said, shaking the water out of his hair, "why didn't you help me?"

"Jamie," she said, "you're the light of my life, but sometimes helping you doesn't seem to help you all that much. You did all right." They walked to the edge of the forest and looked out. Ron and Don, anxious that Jamie might get out of the well somehow, had hired guards to watch for him and had given them a description of what he was wearing. Jamie wasn't sure what he should do.

Just then, a beggar came along, rattling a few coins in a Styrofoam cup. "Any spare change?" he asked.

"I don't have any on me," said Jamie. "But if you like, I'll trade clothes with you." Well, Jamie's clothes were quite nice and the beggar's were mostly rags, so the beggar thought this was a fine idea. They put on each other's clothes, and Jamie walked out past the guards and into his father's kingdom.

"Jamie," said Dorothy, "I'm so impressed! But now we come to a place where you really will need a little help." She ruffled her feathers, turned around several times, and changed herself into a beautiful shop where parrots, cages, and seeds were sold, and groomings were given by appointment only. Jamie was turned into the shop's proprietor. A sign in the window read, "Today only: green parakeets turned back into golden parrots. Inquire within."

After a while, Ron and Don walked by, arguing over whose fault it was that things hadn't turned out right. When they read the sign, they stepped right into the shop, showed their parakeet who was now almost completely featherless to the proprietor, and asked, "Can you really turn this back into a golden parrot? Is it expensive?"

"I don't know, this bird is in terrible condition," the proprietor said, taking the parakeet from them. "But just let me look at it out in the light of day and see if I can do anything. I'll be right back." He walked out of the shop. The moment he did so, the shop changed back into Dorothy, the proprietor once again became Jamie, and the parakeet turned back into the golden parrot with the diamond beak.

"Hello, pretty," it said.

Jamie set the bird on his shoulder and walked to his father's castle with Dorothy. The king was as usual out in his sunflower garden, and he didn't know whether to exult at the sight of the golden parrot or glare because it was on his youngest son's shoulder. Never having had to deal with conflict before, he accepted the parrot in silence. The bird promptly bit him and flew out of reach to the tallest of the sunflowers.

The moment the king received the golden parrot, half of his kingdom immediately became Jamie's. As luck would have it—because luck can have it either way—the coffee shop where Ellery had found work was in

Jamie's half. In the middle of taking an order, Ellery changed from a waiter back into a handsome prince. "—Jamie?" he shouted, completing the question he'd begun back in the forest. Just then, the golden hunting poodle, likewise restored, came bounding into the coffee shop. Patrons scattered. "Find Jamie," Ellery cried, sitting on the poodle's back, and the dog took off, racing to the king's castle so fast that even its shadow was left behind.

Meanwhile, Jamie was telling his father the story of his adventures. The king was growing angrier by the minute. "Impossible," he said. "My sons would never leave anyone down in a well. Not even you." Just then, the golden poodle, Ellery astride it, leapt over the castle walls and into the garden that even now had one or two rosebushes blooming in it from the parrot's droppings.

"It's all true," Ellery declared, as he and Jamie embraced.

"Every word," cried the parrot. "Hello, pretty."

"Lies!" growled the king, disliking the sight of two men embracing in his garden almost as much as he disliked the fragrance of the roses. The golden hunting poodle growled back at him.

"You're going to have to show him, Jamie," said Dorothy, speaking up for the first time in the king's presence. "He always was good at denial."

Jamie called in a loud voice, "Ron and Don, if I let you out, will you confess to everything?"

"Yes," came two muffled voices.

"Dorothy?" Jamie said. She nestled down and laid an egg before the scowling king. When Jamie broke it open, there stood Ron and Don, with egg on their faces. They confessed to everything.

It was a heavy blow to the king's way of looking at things. "Your brothers are included in your half," he said in a shaky voice. "You can punish them in any way you choose."

"Their punishment," Jamie said firmly, "will be to return to their families and live out the remainder of their lives in the stucco duplex."

"Don't!" Ron and Don cried piteously, but it did them no good. Back they went to their wives, children, and stucco duplex, where as it turned out, the rent was due.

So for a while, Jamie and the old king reigned, if not side by side, then at least in the same general proximity. But the old king was badly shaken by the way things had turned out. One day he was in the garden, trying to cheer himself among his sunflowers—which, as it turned out, hadn't been crowded out by the rosebushes and in fact were doing quite well. Ellery, trying to be pleasant, approached him and said, "I love your garden. How did you ever raise such enormous black-eyed Susans?" It was the last straw for the old king. He took off his crown and went into retirement. But whether because he was depressed, or spiteful, or—most likely of all—just plain tired, he left many of the doors in the castle locked when he went. This caused some difficulties for Jamie, who didn't know what the rooms' contents were, but he ruled as best he could.

Some little time after this, Jamie took a walk through his rose-scented kingdom. At the edge of the forest he met Dorothy, whom he hadn't seen much of since he became king. She looked terrible, her feet yellow and scaly, her feathers falling out. "Dorothy," Jamie exclaimed, "what's wrong?"

"You didn't grant my request," Dorothy said in a weak voice. "I'll ask you once more: will you please cut off my head and pluck out my feathers?"

Now that he was king, Jamie understood that he often had to do things he'd rather not. Steeling himself, he did as she asked, cutting off the head of his beloved chicken and plucking out her remaining feathers. No sooner had he done so than there stood before him a pink and portly older gentleman, who would have born a striking resemblance to the old king but for the fact that he was smiling as if the world were a delightful place to live in. "Hello, Jamie, light of my life," laughed the older gentleman. "We've never really met. I'm your Uncle Theodore."

"No," Jamie insisted. "You're my chicken, Dorothy. What have you done with her?"

"Oh, that," replied the older gentleman. "I was—still am, actually—your father's younger brother. He was never really fond of the idea—I was far too different from what he believed the younger brother of a king, or of any man at all, should be. One day, a random word of his, or a lot of words, actually, all of them unpleasant and delivered at a time when I was particularly vulnerable, put a curse on me. Since he thought of me as a man who couldn't do what men should be able to do, the form his curse gave me was of a bird who couldn't fly. He forgot about me entirely. Years passed, and I led a despised, ignominious life. Fortunately, I was a very good layer; otherwise I might have ended up on a serving dish. But then you came along, Jamie, as different from your brothers as I'd been from mine, and I knew I had a chance to be returned to human life. Of course, the tough part was getting you to put an end to the way the old king thought of me. I see now that as long as he continued to rule, you weren't able to do that. But you've become the new king, and here we are."

Well, it was quite a story, but what most impressed Jamie was his uncle. "There was someone like me in the family before," he marveled, and for the first time it seemed to him that he really did belong to a family. Naturally, he invited his Uncle Theodore to come home and live at the castle with him and Ellery. His uncle accepted the invitation with great happiness. When they arrived, Jamie found to his amazement that all those doors left locked by the old king were now open, displaying treasures that had been hidden away for years. The kingdom began to thrive, is thriving still, and Jamie's reign was long and happy.

THE FISHERMAN
AND HIS LOVER

THERE WAS ONCE a very poor fisherman, who had patches on his pants, nothing in his pockets, and only managed to keep food on the table by going down to the sea to catch what he could. But the fisherman had a lover, and like most people who have a lover they're crazy about, he thought the world's riches his own.

Still, he was poor in a material sense and couldn't afford a boat—all he owned was a net. Every morning as the sun came up, he walked down to the edge of the sea, which wasn't far from his tiny but very cozy shack, and waded out into the water. He spent all day every day there, casting his net out and pulling it in, casting it out and pulling it in, until he'd caught enough fish for dinner.

One day at sunset, as he was about ready to head for home, something told the fisherman to cast his net one more time. So he did, and just at that moment a breeze, deciding to leave the land for the sea, filled his net and carried it out much further than usual. The minute he started pulling it back in, the fisherman could tell there was something

"Bajka o Rybaku i Rybce," B (translated for the current author by Andrzej Wilczak); "The Little Sardine," BBFF; "The Fisherman and His Wife," GB.

there, something with a lot of fight in it. Delighted, he hauled the net in hand over hand, and soon whatever he'd caught was thrashing the water to foam with its struggles. When he'd brought it in close enough, he saw that it was a fine fat fish, as long as his arm and red as gold. "We'll eat well off you tonight, my friend," he grunted, getting ready to pull it up onto the sand.

The fish put its head out of the waves, spat the seawater from its mouth, and said, "Release me this instant!"

Well, the fisherman was startled and almost let go of the net. But he regained his composure quickly. "I'm a fisherman," he pointed out, not unreasonably. "You're a fish. You must have been prepared for this possibility."

"I," said the fish, with great dignity, "am not just any fish. I'm the lover of the king of the sea. If I were you, I'd let me go."

It wasn't so much the mention of the fish's connections that helped the fisherman decide to release it as the thought that it—he—had a lover at home who would watch the clock, or whatever they had down there to tell the time, with growing apprehension. He knew how terrible it would be if anything happened to his own lover. Gently, if regretfully, he freed the fish from his net.

"Thank you," the fish said when he was loose. "Now I'd like to return the favor. Tell me what you want, and I'll give it to you."

"That's quite an offer," the fisherman told him. "But I've already got everything I want."

"Lucky you," said the fish. "But it may happen that someday you change your mind about that. If you do, just come down here to the water and call. I'll come." And with a flick of his tail, he was gone.

The fisherman gathered up his catch and took it home. He cleaned and cooked it, as was his custom, because his lover hated to get the smell of fish on his hands. After they ate and the dishes were washed and put away, they made love, which had also become customary. They had been together for a bit over a year, and things had by and large settled into a routine that the fisherman treasured. Afterward, he sat on his side of their bed, inspecting and repairing his net; it was soothing, and he did it each night before going to sleep. "One of the fish I caught today asked me to let him go," he remarked.

His lover, whose name was Kevin, said, "Really? Was it that crunchy little silver one? It had kind of a sharp look in its eye."

"No, silly," the fisherman said fondly. "We didn't eat him. I let him go. He offered me anything in the world I wanted," he added, smiling at the idea.

Kevin set down the magazine he was leafing through. "Did he? So what did we get?"

"Nothing."

"Nothing?" Kevin repeated, his mouth growing thin and hard as a clam's. "You let it go without asking for anything?"

"Well, what's there to ask for?" the fisherman replied, a little uncertain about what Kevin was driving at. He spread his hands to indicate their snug little shack, the bed with its clean sheets, and the two of them in it together: everything in the world anyone could possibly want.

Now, Kevin was very cute. He'd been very cute his entire life, and he'd always cherished the belief that someday he'd end up living in a king's castle or at least be boyfriends with a handsome prince. But Kevin was twenty-eight, and it was beginning to dawn on him that perhaps a fresh fish dinner every night was the most life was going to offer him. It wasn't nearly enough. Completely put out with the fisherman, he snapped, "Why didn't you ask it to give you a bigger cock, you moron!" Then he gave the pillow a vicious punch, threw himself down facing the wall, and went to sleep without another word.

The fisherman was stunned. He'd assumed that Kevin found him as perfect as he found Kevin, and the news that this wasn't so hurt him from one side to the other. He finished repairing his net and turned off the light, but it was a long time before he finally went to sleep. In the morning, when he got up to make coffee, Kevin stayed in bed. This wasn't unusual, but he didn't call to the fisherman to bring him a cup the way he liked it—plenty of milk and sugar and a piece of ice to cool it. Instead he just lay in bed, pretending to be asleep. The fisherman fixed him a cup of coffee anyway and left it for him on the counter, then went out of the house in silence.

All day long as he worked he brooded on Kevin's dissatisfaction with him. When sunset came he laid his net carefully on the sand and waded out into the water. He said,

> "I caught you once
> but set you free;
> come back again
> and speak with me."

Soon the fish put his head out of the waves, spat the seawater from his mouth, and said, "What is it you want?" He was larger than he'd been the day before and looked as if he could simply tear his way out of any net he happened to swim into. The fisherman observed that he seemed to have grown a small pair of horns over his eyes, as well. A little hesitantly, not certain how a fish might take such a request, he said, "Well, it's not for myself that I'm asking but for Kevin. He thinks my cock should be bigger."

The fish didn't even blink. "Go on home," he replied. "Everything has been taken care of." And with a splash of his tail, he was gone.

So the fisherman gathered up his net and his catch and went home. He made dinner, which was eaten in silence. But when they went into their tiny bedroom and undressed and Kevin saw how much larger the fisherman had grown, all was forgiven. They made love as they hadn't since they'd first met. The fisherman was happy, because now every-thing was all right again. But afterward, when he was contentedly mend-ing his net, Kevin smiled at him and said, "Too bad you didn't think to have the fish do something about your nose." Then he settled down, and in three seconds he was asleep.

Well, the fisherman had a nose that went to one side from a fight when he was a boy. Up until now he'd thought it was one of the things that Kevin loved about him, as he loved Kevin's nose for being a little too turned up at the tip—and for being Kevin's nose. And it was a long while before he fell asleep that night.

Next day the fishing was poor. When sunset came the fisherman set his net up on the sand, then waded into the water. He said,

> "I caught you once,"

and soon the fish put his head out of the waves and spat the seawater from his mouth. "What is it you want?" he asked. Today he was even larger, as large as the fisherman himself, and besides having horns, which had also grown, the fish now sported a long barbed tendril on either side of his mouth. The fisherman was a little uncomfortable standing in the water with him. He said, "It's not for myself I'm asking but for Kevin. He thinks my nose should be straighter."

"Go on home," the fish replied. "Everything's been taken care of." And with a slap of his tail that lifted spray into the air, he was gone.

So the fisherman gathered his net and his small catch and went home, made dinner, and called Kevin to the table. When Kevin saw the fisher-man's new nose he was entranced. He kept kissing the fisherman and ad-miring his profile, making him turn this way and that all through dinner. After they'd eaten they went into the bedroom. Kevin was responsive and enthusiastic, and the fisherman said to himself, "Good, he seems happy now; maybe we'll have some peace."

When they'd finished, Kevin gave him a long thoughtful look and said, "Why don't you see what the fish can do about your stomach?" Well, the fisherman was of an age when even though he took good care of himself, his stomach folded over a bit when he sat. It was just one of those things that had to be accepted, or so he'd thought.

He spent a sleepless night, and next day was too tired to fish. He just sat on the shore, brooding until the sun began to set. Then he waded into the water, said,

"I caught you once,"

and soon the fish put his head out of the waves, spat the seawater from his mouth, and asked, "What is it you want?" He was now much larger than the fisherman. Not only had his horns and whiskers lengthened considerably, but row after row of jagged teeth filled his mouth.

The fisherman backed out of the water as tactfully as he could. He explained, "It's not for myself that I ask but for my lover Kevin. He thinks my waist should be slimmer and harder."

"Go on home," the fish replied. "Everything's been taken care of." And with a blow of his tail that soaked the fisherman to the bone, he was gone.

Well, there wasn't much for dinner that night. Kevin didn't notice. He put his hands on the fisherman's waist, which was now like a column of flexible iron, pulled him into their bedroom, and for a little while the fisherman was happy. But when they'd finished, Kevin pulled a clipboard out from under his pillows. He settled himself cross-legged on the bed and began to outline all the changes the fisherman was to request from the fish. Bigger shoulders, thicker thighs, a deeper voice—in fact, if he went along with Kevin's agenda, the fisherman would soon be an entirely new man, and he wasn't sure who. "But then," he said to himself, "this constant changing will be over, and our lives can settle down again." He looked at his Kevin, and all he wanted was to see Kevin's eyes lit up with love for him. If this was what it took, this was what he'd do. So he took the clipboard and began memorizing the items on it.

The next day and every day after that, the fisherman went down to the sea and called the fish. Each time the fish came, he had grown larger and more fearsome than the time before, though he was always amenable to the fisherman's requests. Sometimes the fisherman tried to do a little fishing, but it seemed as if the sea had emptied of all fish but the one. Usually he just sat on the shore and threw stones into the water.

At last the night came when the final item on Kevin's list had been checked off, and the fisherman heaved a sigh of relief. Kevin nestled contentedly on his chest, which was much larger than it had been, and looked up adoringly into his eyes, now a startling shade of blue. "Tomorrow," he murmured, "tell the fish you want a bigger cock." And he fell blissfully asleep.

The fisherman groaned. Gently, so he wouldn't wake him, he slid Kevin off his chest, got dressed, and went out walking into the night. Soon, without thinking, he found himself down at the water. He was tall and broad and heavily muscled, his face was gloriously handsome and he'd never been more miserable in his life. He stood at the edge of the waves and said,

"I caught you once,"

and began to tremble. As if he had been waiting for the fisherman, the fish immediately put his head out of the waves, rising up, and up, and up into the night sky, and spat the seawater from his mouth.

He was now so long that the arches of his back filled the sea like the biggest roller coaster in the world, and his head was a mass of horns and spikes. Two fins fanned out from his spine like vast wings. When he spoke, the words came out in clouds of fire and smoke, though his voice was as gentle as always. "What does he want now?" the fish asked, the huge eyes burning in his head like comets as he looked down at the fisherman.

"I don't know!" the fisherman cried, falling to his knees in despair and confusion—more at Kevin's inconstancy than at the fish's appearance. "I change and I change, and it still doesn't make him happy. I don't know what he wants."

"Go on home," the fish replied. "Everything's been taken care of." And though it seemed there couldn't be enough water in the ocean to cover him, the fish slid back beneath the waves. Steam hissed up in clouds and blew away.

After a while, the fisherman got up off his knees and started home. He couldn't think why—everything was such a mess—but as he walked he began to feel better, lighter. It was just dawn as he reached his shack. He raised his hand to the latch of the door, and then he saw that all the muscle he'd gained was gone. He put his hand to his nose and once again it was pointing to one side. When he looked into his pants, everything there was back to normal as well. The fisherman went inside, wondering how Kevin was going to take this.

To the fisherman's amazement, breakfast was sizzling in a pan on the stove when he walked into the kitchen. Kevin was just pouring two cups of steaming coffee. When he saw the fisherman, his eyes lit up as though the sunrise were taking place just behind them, a sunrise that shone only on the fisherman. "Hi, hon," he said. "We didn't have much in the house, but I scraped something together. I hope it'll be all right—I'm not the world's greatest cook."

The fisherman sat down at the table and sighed gratefully. "Whatever it is," he said, "I'm sure it's perfect." And it was.

THE MAN WHO WAS LOVERS
WITH A PIGEON

THERE WERE ONCE three country boys, brothers, named Tim, Tom, and Howard. They lived in a tiny village where there was nothing to do except work while the sun shone and sleep while it didn't, which didn't suit them at all. The boys dreamed of life in the big city, where there were bright lights all night, streets thronged with traffic, and most important, crowds of people they hadn't known forever.

Now it so happened that they had an Uncle Frank who lived in just such a city, and being fond of his nephews, he invited them to come spend a holiday with him. The three boys had such a good time they decided to make their homes there, if they could find places to live. This was easier said than done, because there was an apartment shortage and rents were ferocious. But eventually each of them found a place for himself—overpriced and cramped, but his own.

The night before they moved out, their Uncle Frank cooked a lavish dinner. After the dishes were cleared away, over coffee and brandy, he

"Petit Jean and the Frog," BBFF; "The Three Feathers," GB; "The Enchanted Frog," GFT; "The Prince Who Married a Frog," IF; "The Frog Princess," RFT; "The Mouse Bride," SFFT.

brought out gifts for his nephews—three plastic disks, of the sort that people throw back and forth in the park on sunny afternoons. Two of the disks were brightly colored, and the third was gray. "Boys," said Uncle Frank, "you're young, and life is the most fun when a person is young. You date, you have adventures, along the way you find out who you are and what you want out of the world. Now, it may be that some-day what you want is one special man to make a life with. But there are so very many men to choose from that finding him may be a problem, and that's where these flying disks will come in handy. All you have to do is close your eyes and throw your disk. Whoever brings it back to you will be your lover." It sounded a little unlikely to the brothers, but their uncle had been so nice that each of them took one of the disks. Tim and Tom, being older, chose first and selected the brightly-colored ones, while Howard was left with the gray. They thanked their uncle for every-thing he'd done for them. Next morning they moved out.

Their lives were happy and very busy as they explored the city and all it offered. As time passed, however, the boys noticed an absence that nothing quite seemed to fill, and that absence was in the form of one spe-cial man. There were certainly crowds of men to meet on the streets, at parties, and while waiting for the rinse cycle to end at the laundromat. They were all very nice, but no one of them seemed to be able to com-pletely fill the absence that Tim, Tom, and Howard each felt in his life. Then they remembered their plastic disks and Uncle Frank's advice.

Tim was the first to try. "All right, here we go," he said, closing his eyes and flinging his disk, which was flame red. A model caught it and brought it back to him. "Here's the man for me," sighed Tim, and off he went with his model.

"Now I'll do it," said Tom, and he closed his eyes and hurled his electric-blue disk. A lawyer caught it and brought it back to him. "He's the one I've been dreaming of," Tom declared, and away he went with his lawyer.

"Am I any different from my brothers?" Howard asked himself, and he also closed his eyes and threw his gray plastic disk. It went into the parking lot of a fast-food restaurant. Howard waited a bit, but when no one brought the disk back to him, he went to see what had happened. It was lying next to a dumpster, and a gray pigeon with red feet was attempting to pick it up with his beak.

When Howard reached down to retrieve the disk and try again, the pigeon said, "Did you lose this?" He puffed out his chest, fanned out his tail, and began to walk around Howard in circles, bowing to him again and again and murmuring in a deep throaty voice. Howard was charmed. And so he became lovers with a pigeon.

Because the pigeon lived under the eaves of a supermarket, where there wasn't really room for two, they decided that he should move in with Howard. He was the perfect lover, attentive, considerate, and he never came home without bringing popcorn or french fries. Still, Howard was a little embarrassed by the relationship—after all, his brothers had gotten a model and a lawyer—and so he never quite got around to telling Tim and Tom that he was lovers with a pigeon. When the three of them met for brunch, Howard never volunteered any information.

"Vito is so gorgeous, all my friends envy me," Tim said blissfully.

"Parker is very successful," said Tom with great satisfaction. "His firm is going to make him a partner."

The two brothers turned to Howard. "And what about your lover?" they asked. "What's his name? What's he do?"

"His name is Columba. Columba Livia," replied Howard, who had looked it up in the public library. "It's a very large family. He's in the restaurant business."

"Oh, a restaurateur," said Tom.

"Interesting name," Tim observed. "Is he Italian?"

When their uncle learned that they all had lovers, he called up each brother to congratulate him, and he made them all a proposal. "Whoever has the most fulfilling relationship will inherit my house. I'd like the three of you to come over for dinner and wear a new outfit that's a gift from your lover." Well, it was a very interesting proposal, because housing was at such a premium in that city that it couldn't be gotten for a model's charm or a lawyer's money. Uncle Frank's house had been built up in the canyons above the city in the days when land was still available, and it was quite large. He'd had offers from contractors and developers that would have allowed him to buy a small country if he'd accepted any of them. But Uncle Frank had put a lot of work into his house and had terraced the face of the canyon below it into gardens that giggled at gravity and gave anyone brave enough to step out on them a view that seemed to reach to the end of the world. So he resisted all offers to sell and dreamed of someday leaving his house to one of his nephews.

When Howard hung up from speaking with his uncle, he heaved a deep sigh. The pigeon, always attentive, said, "What's wrong, hon?"

"I'm invited to my uncle's for dinner," said Howard. "And I'm supposed to wear a new outfit, but I don't have one."

"Is that all?" replied the pigeon. "Here." He plucked a feather from his tail. "Get undressed and put this behind your right ear." Howard did as he was told. When he placed the feather behind his ear, he found himself suddenly dressed in a perfectly tailored gray suit, which gleamed subtle purples and greens where the light hit it, and a pair of scarlet shoes. "You look great in that," the pigeon told him. Howard thanked him and left for his uncle's.

When he got there, he found Tim dressed in next season's Paris suit, the gift of his lover the model. Tom was wearing a very expensive Italian suit, given to him by his lover the lawyer. But his own iridescent gray suit outshone them both. "Love those red shoes, Howard," said Uncle

Frank. He noted the pigeon feather behind his nephew's ear. "So, boys, how are the relationships going?" Everyone said the relationships were going just fine. But when Uncle Frank went into the kitchen to see about dinner, the two older brothers told a different story.

"Vito's always traveling around the world on modeling assignments," Tim complained.

"Parker's always at work," mourned Tom. "I'm an office widow."

"And what about Columba?" the two brothers asked Howard. "How's it going, *really?*"

"Well, pretty good," Howard said. "We spend a lot of time together." Tim and Tom told him how happy they were for him, and didn't speak to him for the rest of the night.

As they were leaving, their uncle said, "Come to dinner again tomorrow night. I want each of you to show me something your lover has taught you to do that you couldn't do before."

When Howard got home, the pigeon asked, "How was the dinner?"

"Good," Howard answered. "My uncle liked the suit you gave me best." But he was very sad and preoccupied. The pigeon tenderly preened his hair the way Howard liked and asked him what was wrong. Finally Howard said, "I've been invited to dinner again tomorrow night. This time I have to show him something you've taught me to do, and all I can think of is that dance you do when you're glad to see me."

"That's fun," the pigeon laughed, "but I can teach you to do something even better than that." He plucked a feather from his tail and gave it to Howard. "Put this behind your left ear and do as I do," he said, fluttering his wings and taking flight around the room. So Howard put the feather behind his ear, flapped his arms, and flew. Unfortunately, the room was very small, and his flight was interrupted by the wall. He fell to the floor in a heap. "You're a natural at it," the pigeon soothed him. "You just need a little practice."

Next evening the three brothers met at their uncle's house. "This is what Vito taught me to do," Tim said. He stepped over to the swimming pool and gave it a look of such disdain and dismissal that the chlorinated water froze solid.

"Well, this is what I've learned from Parker," said Tom. He stood in front of his uncle's couch, which was upholstered with black material, and by closely reasoned logic and misrepresentation of the facts, he began proving that actually it wasn't black at all. By the time he summed up his argument, the couch was white.

"Very impressive, boys," said Uncle Frank. "Howard? It's your turn. What has Columba taught you to do?"

"This," said Howard, stepping off the edge of the terrace to a fanfare of gasps from his brothers. He flew away out over the city until he was just a speck, circled the tallest buildings, and returned.

"Astonishing," said Uncle Frank. "Now that's something worth learning to do." He noticed the pigeon feather behind Howard's ear but didn't say anything. "Make yourselves at home," he said. "I'll go get dinner."

When he left the room, Tim and Tom began grousing about their lovers. "Vito sleeps around *a lot*," Tim griped.

"Parker treats me like his houseboy. He expects me to serve drinks when he brings people home from the office," growled Tom.

They turned to Howard. "Come on," they wheedled. "You can tell us how Columba treats you. Terribly, right?"

"Well, no, not really," Howard said. "When he sees me, he bows to me and does a dance."

"A dance?" his brothers asked. "What kind of a dance?"

"It always makes me think of a minuet from the court of Louis XIV," Howard told them. Tim and Tom said that sounded really adorable and ground their teeth.

When their uncle was seeing them to the door, he said, "Boys, I've almost made up my mind who's going to get the house. Come to dinner tomorrow, and bring your lovers so I can meet them."

"What am I going to do now?" Howard asked himself as he flew home. He didn't see how he could possibly bring the pigeon to his uncle's, not if his brothers were bringing a model and a lawyer. He thought perhaps he might hire someone to play the part of Columba the following evening.

"How was it?" the pigeon asked when he flew in the window.

"It was really good," Howard replied. The pigeon could see that once again something was bothering Howard, but no matter how he preened him, Howard wouldn't talk about it. "Tomorrow," he promised.

But in the morning Howard went out on some errands. In the afternoon he passed by the fast-food restaurant where they'd first met, and there was the pigeon, eating french fries off the ground with the other pigeons. "It's now or never," Howard told himself, and he stopped.

The pigeon came over immediately. "Hi, hon," he cooed.

"Hi," said Howard. "We need to talk." The pigeon nodded and waited for him to begin. At last Howard said, "My uncle wants us to bring our lovers to dinner tonight so he can meet them. That way he can decide whom he's going to leave his house to."

"Uh-huh," said the pigeon.

"My brother Tim has a model for a lover, and Tom has a lawyer," Howard continued.

"Aren't they lucky," observed the pigeon.

Just then, who should come out of the fast-food restaurant but Tim and Tom. They'd been commiserating about their terrible luck with lovers, but when they saw Howard and the pigeon engaged in an intimate conversation, their faces lit up like Saturday and Sunday morning. "Don't tell me *this* is the mystery boyfriend," Tim crowed.

"Oh, Howard, you can do better than *that*," Tom whispered loudly, delighted that Howard hadn't.

"See you two lovebirds tonight at Uncle's," the two brothers chorused, walking away with light hearts. Howard couldn't even look at the pigeon.

"Howard," the pigeon said gently. "This isn't about your brothers or your uncle, is it? It's about you and me. You're embarrassed by me because I'm a pigeon."

"You're right," Howard admitted, disgusted with himself. "I envy my brothers because their lovers are handsome and successful, even though Vito and Parker are such reptiles." He shook himself. "Well, if they can be with reptiles, why in the world shouldn't I love a pigeon who's as good to me as you are? We're going to my uncle's for dinner tonight. I love you, and I don't care what anybody thinks about it."

"All right then!" cried the pigeon happily, fluttering his wings. "Let's go in style!" He flew into the dumpster behind the restaurant and found four plastic lids and two straws, with which he made some wheels. When he set a Styrofoam burger container on top of them, presto! he had a carriage. Then he harnessed a mouse who lived in back of the dumpster to the carriage with two straw wrappers, and he was ready to go. "I'm sorry the carriage isn't big enough for you, too," he apologized. "But you can walk beside it." And so they set off.

Well, no matter how slowly Howard walked, the pigeon in his mouse-drawn carriage kept falling behind. Finally Howard sat down on a bus bench to give the pigeon time to catch up, but he was so long in coming that Howard fell asleep. At last the little trash carriage came rolling along in the gutter. As it passed him, it turned into a glittering limousine a block long and the mouse became a blond chauffeur. The pigeon changed into the most handsome man in the world, and he was wearing a beautiful gray suit, which gleamed purple and green where the light touched it, and a pair of scarlet shoes. The limousine left Howard snoring gently on the bus bench and sped up into the hills to his uncle's house.

When the handsome man walked in, Vito was on the terrace staring moodily out at the city while Tim watched him. Parker was taking an important call on his cellular phone while Tom waited for him to finish. The handsome man introduced himself to Uncle Frank. "Hello," he said. "I'm Columba Livia, Howard's lover."

Tim and Tom stormed over when they heard this. As they did, Vito happened to glance over at Parker and gave him a glossy full-page smile. Parker told his caller he'd have to get back to him and hung up.

"You're not Howard's lover," Tim accused.

"No?" Columba asked. "Are you sure?"

"Positive," stated Tom. "We met Howard's lover, and he's a pigeon."

Columba drew their attention to the front door, where Vito and Parker were making a discreet exit together. "I'd say the only pigeons around here were you two," he said quietly. Tim and Tom gave a cry of dismay and ran out after their inconstant lovers.

Meanwhile, Howard woke up on his bus bench, didn't see the pigeon and his carriage either behind him or before him, and hurried to his uncle's house. When he got there, he found his uncle and the most handsome man he had ever seen out on the terrace, chatting together as if they'd known one another for years.

"Uncle Frank," said Howard, "has a pigeon come here? Where are Tim and Tom? Who are you?" This last was directed to the handsome man, who was smiling at him radiantly.

"If you don't recognize me, Howard, surely you recognize the gray suit and red shoes," said Columba.

Howard did. "Really," he said in amazement, sitting down. "What happened?"

"You loved me," Columba said.

"And freed you from an evil spell, right?" Howard finished for him.

"Well, no, not really," Columba replied. "I've always been a pigeon. But when you loved me, you changed me."

"I had a feeling you'd done well for yourself, Howard," said Uncle Frank. "And I was right—Columba here has been singing your praises all afternoon. I'd be delighted to think that this house was going to be the setting for such a love, so I've decided that it will go to you. Actually, the two of you could move in now, if you like—there's more than enough room." And he excused himself out to the kitchen to see about dinner.

Howard looked at Columba and smiled shyly. "You're really handsome," he said. "But I don't know. I kind of got used to you as a pigeon."

Columba leaned forward and began to preen Howard's hair with his mouth, tenderly, the way he knew Howard liked. "I just *look* different, hon," he cooed in his low throaty voice. "Underneath, I'm still the same pigeon you fell in love with." And Howard realized this was true.

THE UGLY DUCKLING

THERE WAS ONCE a brown duckling who lived with his brothers and sisters on the edge of a small pond. In his heart, he didn't feel as if he were in the right family, and in their hearts, his family agreed. They shared this feeling with him as occasion permitted, which, as things worked out, was on a daily basis. They were critical of the way he swam: "*That's* not how a duck's supposed to swim, stupid." They were critical of the way he groomed his feathers: "That's *not* how a duck's supposed to look, ugly." Sometimes it was "stupid," sometimes "ugly,"—but always something and always unpleasant. Now, he couldn't stand his brothers and sisters, so he knew he wasn't stupid. But, oh! he felt ugly: the ugly duckling. He spent most of his time out on the pond, as far from the others as he could get, and he had an active fantasy life.

One morning as he floated alone, dreaming a favorite dream ("Hollywood Signs Ugly Duckling! Family Purchased by Chinese Restaurant!"), there was a flurry of white wings, and a stranger splashed down not too far from him. The stranger settled his feathers, nodded to the ugly duckling, and said, "Hello, there. Nice day." The ugly duckling was speechless—he had never seen anyone so handsome in his life. It wasn't just the other bird's plumage (aristocratic), his wings (massive), or his neck

"The Ugly Duckling," HCA.

(how could *anyone* have such a neck, so sinuous, so graceful, so totally unducklike?), though these were a revelation of what a bird could be. But it was the way the stranger carried himself that captivated the duckling, as if terrible things had given him wonderful gifts—compassion from grief, courage from fear, patience and serenity from sorrow. After a short while, the handsome stranger sighed and said, "Well, my friend, I still have a long way to go. Thank you for your hospitality." Beating the air with his amazing wings, he ran across the water and took off into the sky again.

"Hello," murmured the ugly duckling, regaining his tongue. Then he shook himself and cried, "Why, of course! That's who I am, or who I'm supposed to be. Somehow I've been raised in the wrong nest, which explains why all those so-called brothers and sisters of mine are always so unpleasant." He determined not to waste a moment but to leave immediately and catch up with the handsome stranger. And away he flew without a good-bye to his family.

Although the stranger hadn't seemed to get much of a head start, the ugly duckling now couldn't see him anywhere. He flew on and on in the direction the other bird had taken. Days passed and then weeks. The ugly duckling stopped at every pond and stream he found, but the handsome stranger was never there. At last his search took him to a lake, vaster than anything he could have dreamed. Flocks of every kind of bird crowded the shores calling to each other, sailed across the water, or circled in the air. "If he's not here," said the ugly duckling to himself above the tumult, "then he's the only bird in the world who isn't, and sooner or later he's bound to show up." He flew down to the lake and proceeded to make a place for himself among its crowds.

At first many of the birds seemed strange and even bizarre to the ugly duckling, who only knew ducks. But slowly they became familiar to him. There were the eagles, who perched alone on the treetops and never spoke to anyone, though whenever one was spotted everyone would murmur, "Look, look: an eagle," and there would be much preening of plumage and spreading of tails. There were the flamingos, so elegant, so poised, but always posing at the edge of things, exchanging acrid remarks with one another. There were the wild geese, not very bright but loyal in their friendships, and the seagulls, who flew in from the ocean miles away, looking for parties. There were even ducks, but the ugly duckling made a point of ignoring them.

He realized of course that he wasn't worthy of the handsome stranger in his present condition, and so he began a daily regimen of exercise to improve himself. Each day began with an hour of aerobics and yoga, intended to increase the length and suppleness of his neck. Then followed an exhaustive workout, focused on his wings. He took in massive amounts of protein and carbohydrates, got plenty of sleep, and even considered taking steroids for a while, until he heard some unpleasant stories about the mood swings associated with them. Because he was so dedicated, results began to show, and he was soon a splendid specimen of a waterfowl. Unfortunately, he didn't look any more like the handsome stranger than he had before he began. So, as far as he was concerned, he was still an ugly duckling.

One morning, as he meditated out on the water, psyching himself up for his laps around the lake, someone said, "Hello, there." The ugly duckling spun around, certain it was the handsome stranger, arriving at last. But no, it was only a little blue loon, who had paddled over to introduce himself. The ugly duckling was bitterly disappointed—would the handsome stranger *never* show up?—and consequently less than cordial.

But the loon wasn't put off by his gruffness. He struck up a conversation and was so charming, with such an odd sense of humor, that soon the ugly duckling was laughing. This wasn't something that happened often. Next day they happened to run into each other, and the following day as well. The loon asked for some advice on exercise; he knew of a little spot out on the lake where the fish had very low fat content; he'd heard the sunset was going to be particularly beautiful that evening and did the ugly duckling want to go see it together? They began keeping regular company, meeting for lunch or to work out. The loon teased him, saying, "You look great. I don't see why you push yourself so hard." But the ugly duckling knew how far short he fell of his ideal, and he only pushed harder.

One morning the loon was late. The ugly duckling was about to take off for his daily set of laps around the lake—today he was going to move his total up to twenty, and his adrenaline was high—when the loon paddled over in a considerable state of excitement himself. One of the nests on the fashionable west shore of the lake had fallen vacant, and the loon wanted to know if the ugly duckling was interested in becoming roommates. The ugly duckling didn't mind.

So they moved in together. It was a considerable change of lifestyle for the ugly duckling. Since his arrival he had been too busy with his self-improvement program to make any friends, but it seemed there wasn't a bird on the lake who didn't know the loon and like him. There were nest-warming parties and potlucks and shopping excursions for just the right cattails to fill that spot in the corner. The loon seemed very happy. But in his heart, the ugly duckling always kept an empty place for the handsome stranger, who one day would come to take him away. Meantime, the loon was pleasant company to kill time with.

It happened one morning that when the ugly duckling went in to wake his roommate, the loon said, "I'm kind of bushed. I think I'll sleep in." They'd had guests the night before who'd stayed late. The ugly duckling thought nothing of it and said, "OK. I'm going to go work out." When he got back that afternoon, the loon was still in bed.

Next morning it was the same story. The loon said, "I'm just really tired. You go on without me." And suddenly the ugly duckling was worried. Everyone knew there was an illness going around the lake, that it was almost always fatal, and one of its symptoms was fatigue.

"Are you sure you're all right?" he asked. But the loon turned away and didn't answer.

The ugly duckling went down to the lake and began his yoga, but the thought of the loon lying alone kept breaking his concentration. "I guess it won't hurt me to skip just one day," he said to himself. So he caught some minnows for the loon's breakfast, brought them back to the nest, and spent the day sitting with his friend.

Now began a difficult time for the ugly duckling, who had never taken care of anyone before. Some days the loon felt as good as ever, and the two of them went down to the water. Other days the loon was sick, and the ugly duckling sat with him, only leaving to bring his friend something to eat. The ugly duckling was afraid and wanted to cover his head with his wings but couldn't, because the loon needed comforting and tending. He wanted to give in to bitterness, and resentment, and despair but couldn't, because if he did he would miss the odd moments of gratitude that came suddenly and unannounced. Gratitude that some days the loon felt a little stronger, that his friend wasn't alone, that he was the one who was there for him. Under the circumstances, gratitude seemed very strange, but it refreshed and strengthened him when it came, and he couldn't afford to miss it.

Sometimes friends stopped by to visit. Then the ugly duckling would take the opportunity to fly across the lake and far back into the swamps. There, he sought out owls or cranes, any bird reputed to have discovered a cure, or at least a treatment, for the illness. Sometimes he brought back mistletoe, sometimes strange-looking mushrooms, sometimes licorice or purple echinacea flowers or cat's claw, and gave these to the loon. Then the two of them would wait to see if anything helped. Some things did, a bit.

One night the loon came down with a fever. He'd had them before, of course, but this time it felt like he was being roasted from the inside. The ugly duckling brought him willow bark, and though this was usually helpful in lowering temperatures, it had no effect. He sat up with the loon all night, giving him water, tucking him in with soft grasses, watching and waiting. His friend seemed to be delirious at one point. "This is very nice of you," he muttered, as the ugly duckling lifted his head to give him a drink. "But have we met before?" At last, a little before dawn, the loon's fever broke, and he recognized the ugly duckling again. "Why, it's you," he mumbled, then relaxed into a deep natural sleep. The ugly duckling thought it would be a good idea to have something on hand for breakfast, in case the loon wanted anything to eat when he woke. He slipped quickly away down to the lake.

It was that moment just before day catches up with night. The night birds had all gone to sleep, the day birds weren't awake yet, and the lake was still and unbroken. As the ugly duckling reached its edge, the first light of the new day flew up over the tops of the trees and lit the sky, so his reflection suddenly appeared on the water's surface. What was that he saw? Not the massive wings or elegant neck or snowy plumage he'd longed for, but someone who carried himself as if terrible things were giving him wonderful gifts—compassion from grief, courage from fear, patience and serenity from sorrow. Then the duck, who was neither a duckling nor ugly any longer, gathered some food for his friend's breakfast and brought it back to their nest.

And that
is where the two of them are
right now.

GODFATHER DEATH

THERE WAS ONCE a man who had twelve children, and when the thirteenth was born the man didn't know what to do. The times were hard, the times were bad, and the man had no friends or relatives who weren't already godparent to one of his other children. It was Friday evening and next morning his son had to be baptized. In despair, the man rushed out into the street, determined to ask the first person he met to be his son's godfather.

He hadn't waited long when a very distinguished older gentleman with a flowing white beard approached him. "I've heard about your problem," the older gentleman said, in a grand but benign manner, "and I'm willing to be the boy's godfather."

"That's certainly very nice of you," the man said. "Please, who are you?"

"Why, son, don't you recognize me?" the older gentleman chided him gently. "It's me, the Lord."

The man wasn't impressed. "No, thanks," he replied. "The world goes from bad to worse to completely impossible, and what are you doing about it—waiting for an opportune moment? No, I think my son

"The Woman with Three Children," BBFF; "Godfather Death," "The Godfather," and "Mother Trudy," GB; "Death and the Doctor," SFFT.

can do a little better than you for a godfather. Be on your way." The older gentleman sighed and left.

In a little while, a handsome young gentleman with a very well-manicured beard approached the man. "I've heard of your problem," said the handsome gentleman, "and here I am, ready to be the boy's godfather."

"I'm much obliged," the man said. "Please, who are you?"

"Now, now, don't be coy," the handsome gentleman said, grinning at him. "You know me—I'm the Devil."

The man began to grow impatient. "I don't think so," he said. "People work hard to cheat and betray and kill each other, and after it's all done you show up and try to claim credit for it. What kind of godfather is that for my son? Be on your way." The handsome gentleman went off very disturbed, not being used to rejection.

In a little while a third gentleman approached the man. He was of indeterminate age and had no beard at all, no hair on top of his head, and no eyebrows. "I've heard of your problem," the hairless gentleman said. "I'll be the boy's godfather."

"Maybe you will, and maybe you won't," the man replied. "Who are you?"

"We've never met," said the hairless gentleman. "I'm Death."

"Well, now," said the man. He glanced up the street, but no one else was coming. So he turned the offer over in his mind a time or two and at last said, "You're a hard worker. And you don't carry a grudge. Even though you don't receive many invitations, you still pay everyone a visit. Yes, I think you'll make a fine godfather for my son."

So next day the hairless gentleman showed up at the church and held the boy during his christening. His parents named him Martin. After the baptism was over, the hairless gentleman took the man aside and said, "When the boy comes of age, send him to me at my house, and I'll see what I can do for him." Then he left.

Martin grew as his brothers and sisters grew, neither faster nor slower. On his eighteenth birthday, his father said to him, "It's time you met your godfather. Go across the city to such and such an address and introduce yourself." Martin went.

When he got to the address, he didn't care for the looks of it. It was an old office building with one of its walls torn away and nothing around it for blocks but empty parking lots. But he went inside and there was a staircase. He climbed one flight of stairs, and there on the first landing was a barbell. It was pumping itself up and down, up and down without stopping.

"Excuse me, is this where my godfather lives?" Martin asked.

The barbell paused in midair. "One flight up," it grunted. Martin walked around it and walked up another flight.

On the second landing he found a brand-new pair of jeans and a full-length mirror. They were having a bitter disagreement that had come to blows. "Excuse me, is this where my godfather lives?" Martin asked.

The jeans and the mirror paused in their fight. "One flight up," they told him. Martin walked around them and went up another flight.

On the third landing he came upon a large bottle of whiskey, a small bottle of poppers, and a tiny bottle of cocaine. They had their arms around one another's shoulders and were singing all the old songs together. "Excuse me, is this where my godfather lives?" Martin asked.

"One flight up," the three bottles sang in harmony. Martin walked around them and climbed another flight.

At the fourth landing he found himself confronted with a closed door. From behind it there came the rasp, rasp, rasp of something being sharpened. Martin put his eye to the keyhole and looked inside. A skeleton sat on a bench, honing the blade of a scythe with a whetstone. Martin really didn't want to interrupt the skeleton to inquire after his godfather, and so he backed away from the door. But he stepped on a loose floorboard, and it creaked. Immediately a voice called from behind the door, "Martin, is that you? Come on in, it's open." So Martin went in.

He found himself in a light, spacious office decorated in neutral tones, with a view of the entire city. A hairless gentleman sat behind a desk, reviewing a stack of what seemed to be birth certificates. "Hello, Martin," the hairless gentleman said. "I'm your godfather. Did you have any trouble finding the place?"

Martin said, "No, but I saw so many strange things on the stairs. There was a barbell pumping itself up and down."

"Oh, Martin," his godfather laughed, dismissing such a fantasy. "The light's not very good on the stairs. That was my weight trainer."

"Well," Martin said, "on the second landing I saw a pair of jeans and a mirror fighting."

"That was my tailor and his model. I'm afraid the model is putting on a little weight and doesn't like to admit it."

"I saw a bottle of whiskey, a bottle of poppers, and a bottle of cocaine singing together on the third landing," Martin said.

"I belong to a barbershop quartet," his godfather smiled. "Anything else?"

"Godfather, when I got up here, I looked in the keyhole and saw a skeleton sharpening the blade of a scythe."

His godfather stopped smiling. "That was me in my work clothes. Please, Martin, do have a seat. Now. Have you given any thought to how you'll make your living?"

"Well," Martin said, "I thought I might like to be a doctor."

"Some of my best friends are," said his godfather. He opened a drawer, took out a small bottle of something colorless, and set it on the desk between them. "It's just water, really," he told Martin. "But with a drop of this, you can cure anyone of anything. It should come in quite handy. But listen, doctor. When you go into a patient's room, I want you to look for me. If I'm standing by your patient's head, I've just come for a visit, and you may administer the water. But if you see me standing at the patient's feet, then I'm there on business, and you're to shake your head very sadly and say there's nothing medical science can do. And Martin? Don't ever give the water to anyone I've already claimed. Don't ever oppose me: I'm your godfather." He stood to put the bottle in Martin's hand, and as he did his shadow rose up behind him. It was much larger than it should have been, and though Martin stared, he couldn't see anything in it, anything at all. This was especially disturbing because the shadow was covering part of a window.

"Oh, and before I forget: that bottle does have one other quality," his godfather said, walking Martin to the door. "As long as you have it, I won't be paying a business call on you. So good to have seen you. We really must have lunch together just as soon as my schedule permits."

"Yes, sure, anytime you like. Thank you very much," Martin said, and when the door closed behind him he raced down the stairs and out of the building as fast as he could.

So Martin set up an office for himself, and in a very short while his fame as a physician spread, not least because he was one of the few doctors who made house calls. When he entered a patient's room, he looked to see if his godfather was there. When Martin saw him next to the patient's head, he took out his bottle of water, administered a drop, and the cure was miraculous. But when his godfather was at the patient's feet, Martin shook his head and said, "I'm sorry. You've called me too late."

Now it happened that the kingdom was visited by an epidemic, and Martin was busy all hours of the day. One night a messenger from the king came to his office. The king's son was ill, and not only couldn't the court physicians find the cure in any of their books, they couldn't even find the name of the illness. Martin accompanied the messenger to the palace. There, he was shown to the bedroom of the king's son, and all the physicians made way for him.

The king's son was unconscious when Martin arrived. Even so, he was the most beautiful young man Martin had ever seen, and all he could do was stare. The king approached Martin and said, "If you can make my son well, I'll make you wealthier than your wildest dreams."

Well, Martin was a very successful doctor, and his wealth had surpassed his wildest dreams some time ago. He said, "I'll cure your son, but what I ask as a reward is that he and I pledge our hearts to each other."

Now, the king wasn't pleased with this answer. But he reflected that his son's life was what mattered most to him. He said, "That'll be my son's decision to make. But if he smiles on you, I won't stand in the way."

Martin said, "That's fair enough." Just then his godfather slipped into the room and took his position by the feet of the king's son. He shook his head at Martin. But Martin looked at the king's son and thought, I've never seen anyone like him before. And so, quickly, he turned the king's son around in the bed so that his head was at the foot and his feet were on the pillow, and gave him a drop of water from the bottle. The king's son opened his eyes, and the first person he saw was Martin. He smiled. But the godfather glared at Martin and walked out of the room.

The king saw the way his son smiled at Martin, and he said, "You've cured my son and I'll keep my word. I won't stand in your way." But remembering the look his godfather had given him, Martin was uneasy and not at all certain about the cure.

Toasts were drunk to the health of the king's son and to Martin's skill as a doctor. It was long past midnight when Martin got back to his office. His godfather was waiting for him in his bare bones, and his shadow behind him was enormous. Martin was terrified. He threw himself on his knees. "I'm sorry," he cried. "I'll never do it again. Forgive me." He wept and he begged, and at last his godfather relented.

"Martin," he said. "everyone makes a mistake once, and I'll forgive you once. I'll be back for the king's son sooner or later, as my schedule

permits. Next time, you are not to oppose me. Because look, Martin."
He pointed a bony finger back at his shadow. It was deep and dark, and
whatever it fell on disappeared. His godfather reached down around his
ankles and pulled his flesh and suit back on, gave Martin a last sharp
look, and left the office.

All Martin wanted to do now was to avoid his godfather. He reasoned
that the best way to do this would be by avoiding all his patients, and especially the king's son. The next day whenever anyone came to his office, he refused to answer the door. He refused to answer the door the
following day as well. But on the third day, the king's son came to see
him, and against his better judgment Martin let him in.

They sat on the couch together, and the king's son was so glad to see
Martin, so radiant with health, that Martin said to himself, Surely my
godfather isn't coming for him. Soon they embraced, and the king's son
pledged his heart to Martin, and Martin pledged his in return. For many
days they were happy together, though Martin still refused to practice
his profession.

But a night came when Martin was awakened by a messenger from
the palace. The king's son had fallen ill again, none of the doctors could
help him, and Martin had to come right away. Martin dressed and went
with the messenger.

When he got there, the king's son was unconscious. An IV drip of
clear fluid ran into him and a catheter ran out of him, and even though a
tube of oxygen hissed in his nostrils, he breathed as if his lungs were
fighting a losing battle with the air. The godfather stood at his feet, and
when he looked up and saw Martin he held up his hand, forbidding
Martin to enter. Martin might have done so anyway. But behind his godfather rose the shadow, and no matter how he stared into it he could see
nothing, so that he couldn't tell if the shadow had an end or if it went on
forever. He sat down on the threshold of the room, hid his face in his
hands, and began to cry.

Someone in the room spoke. When Martin raised his face, he saw that his crying had awakened the king's son, who was trying to speak. "What?" Martin asked, trying to make it out.

"Don't be afraid," whispered the king's son. "It's all right."

So Martin groaned, got to his feet, and entered the room, brushing past his godfather. He lifted the king's son in his arms and, with difficulty because of all the tubes, turned him around on the bed so his head was at the foot. Then he gave him a drop of water from the bottle. But his godfather glared at him and stepped to the other end of the bed, so that once again he was at the feet of the king's son. Martin turned him around again. All night long the three of them performed a strange dance. At last the godfather was overcome with frustration and stormed out of the room. The king's son began to breathe a little more easily. Martin needed a cigarette, but because the oxygen was still on, he stepped out into the hallway.

He had just put the cigarette in his mouth and was about to light it when his godfather appeared before him. He was in his bare bones, and behind him the shadow seemed to have swallowed the palace, and the city, and the sky with its stars. "Martin," he hissed. "This is the second time you've defied me, and I only forgive the first time."

Martin was more tired than he would have believed possible, and he really wanted a cigarette. He wasn't thinking all that well. All he knew was that in spite of all his efforts, here was his godfather, still so close to the king's son. "Get *out* of here!" he snarled, and putting his hands on the skeleton's rib cage, he shoved it back with all his might. Now, no one had ever laid hands on him before, and the godfather was taken by surprise. He actually backed up a step—just one, and then he set his feet and couldn't be budged. But an odd thing happened. As Martin exerted all his strength against his godfather, a tiny bit of the shadow slipped into his mouth, and he swallowed it. Now he found that he could see into the shadow, and when he saw what he saw, he was no longer afraid of it.

Meanwhile, his godfather was very offended by this rough treatment. "Martin," he demanded, holding out his boney hand. "Give me back my bottle of water."

"Take it," replied Martin. "Take it, and I'll give him whatever water I can distill for him in my own heart."

"Of course you realize this means you'll have to go into the shadow, the same as everyone else."

"That's right. The same as everyone else."

"Oh, Martin," sighed the godfather. "I had such high hopes for you—I was even thinking of making you my partner. But now, I wash my hands of you. From now on, you're on your own.

"No, I'm not," said Martin. "I'm with the king's son." And he left the godfather standing out in the hall and went back inside to be with the man he loved.

PENNY LOAFERS

THERE WAS ONCE a young man named Jeffrey who fell in love with a furniture maker named George, and after dating and courtship and breaking apart and making up the two of them decided to move in together. Jeffrey lived in a one-bedroom apartment, while George had a lovely house furnished with all his finest pieces, so Jeffrey came to live with George. And for quite a long while, they were very happy.

But George became ill, and after getting worse, getting better, and then getting much worse, he died. He died at ten o'clock in the morning and didn't leave a will. At ten forty-five, his three sisters who hadn't spoken to him in many years arrived at the door with three trucks, and by the time the sun set, George's lovely house was empty. The three sisters even took George's pets, though none of them was an animal lover. But as they said to one another, "blood is thicker than water," by which they meant that Jeffrey should be left with nothing. But one dog was so old, so decrepit, that none of the sisters could bring herself to take him. His fur was gone in great pink patches of skin, his testicles were swollen, and he limped along slowly with his nose and his ears on the ground. So he was left behind.

Jeffrey sat in what had been the bedroom and cried. He cried because his lover had suffered, and because now he was alone, and because it

"The Master Cat, or Puss in Boots," AL; "Puss in Boots," GB; "Puss in Boots," PCFT.

takes so little time for the world to turn upside down. But soon he had to put crying away and try to think. Next day the house would be sold and the money shared among the three sisters; Jeffrey had nowhere to go, no way to earn a living, and was no longer as young as he had once been. He got to his feet and wandered from room to room of the empty house to see if anything had been left to him.

When he came to the very last room, there lay the dog no one had wanted. "What am I going to do with you?" Jeffrey asked sadly, looking down at him.

The dog considered the matter. "Buy me a pair of penny loafers," he suggested.

Well, as you can imagine, the dog's answer took Jeffrey by surprise, because of course he'd been asking what was he to do with himself, not what was he to do with the dog. But once he'd found his voice, the dog was persistent. "I'm serious," he said. "Buy me a pair of penny loafers. And not in black. I want them in red."

Well, Jeffrey pulled out his wallet and saw he still had a few dollars. He shrugged. "I feel like my heart's gone out of my chest," he sighed. "Why not buy a pair of shoes for a dog? I'll take you out tomorrow, and we'll get you some." That night, Jeffrey slept on the bare floor, but his head was pillowed on the dog that no one wanted.

Next morning he left the house for the last time and walked to a shoe store. "I'll wait out here," the dog said. Jeffrey went inside and bought the smallest pair of penny loafers the shoe clerk had, the smallest Jeffrey had ever seen, and they were red. When he paid for them, the only change he got back was two cents. He took the shoes out to the dog. "Can you give me a hand with them?" the dog asked. Jeffrey knelt down and slipped the loafers on the dog's back paws. "Something's missing," the dog said. "They're not quite right." Jeffrey took the two pennies out of his pocket and slipped one into the slot in the upper of each shoe.

The dog stood up on his hind legs and took a few steps up and down the sidewalk. "Great!" he said approvingly. "Great, great, great!" And what a difference came over him! His fur grew back thick and sleek, his testicles shrank to a more becoming size, and his ears perked right up. The first thing he did was to take Jeffrey by the arm and walk him to a nearby park, where he sat him down on a bench that was partly in the sun, partly in the shade. "I'm going to go get us something to eat," he said. "Are you going to be all right if I leave you here?" Jeffrey just shrugged and nodded.

The dog went through the park and gathered an enormous bouquet of every kind of flower that grew there. Then he quickly carried the bouquet across town to the tall building where the prince had his penthouse offices. A security guard in a brown blazer stood at the door. "No dogs allowed in the lobby," he said.

"Quite right," the dog said approvingly. "You run a tight, no-nonsense operation here, and I'm sure the prince will be very glad to hear that. But these flowers were picked not ten minutes ago on the estate of the wealthy and powerful Jeffrey as a gift for the prince. Frankly, if I don't deliver them before they wilt, I fear for your job."

Well, jobs were scarce and the security guard was very insecure about his, so he said, "I can give you a visitor's pass. It'll get you as far as the prince's receptionist, but you'll have to deal with her yourself."

"Thank you," the dog said. "Can you get the door for me?" The dog crossed the lobby and rode the elevator up to the penthouse. He stopped in front of the receptionist's desk. "Flowers for the prince," he said.

The receptionist looked up from her magazine. "All deliveries go to the mail room on the sixteenth floor," she said; she didn't like being bothered.

"As well they should," the dog agreed. "But these flowers were picked on the estate of the wealthy and powerful Jeffrey not ten minutes ago, and if the dew dries on their petals before the prince gets them . . . Well. I just fear for your job."

The receptionist was every bit as scared of unemployment as the security guard. "I can buzz you through to the prince's private secretary," she said. "But you'll have to deal with him yourself if you want to see the prince."

"By all means, buzz me through," the dog said. The receptionist did. The dog stopped in front of the desk of the prince's private secretary. "Flowers for the prince," he said.

The private secretary glanced up from the document he was reading and looked the dog over. "One moment, please," he said, and stepped into the prince's luxurious office.

Now, the prince was at that stage of life—that is, between puberty and death—where he might have benefited from a romantic attachment. The only difficulty was that he was very easily bored. This could be an intimidating trait in any dinner companion, but when that dinner companion was a prince it meant the evening might end with a long stay in the dungeon on bread and water. Because of this, not many men were willing to risk asking the prince out, nor had they been for quite some time, and he was getting edgy and dissatisfied. The private secretary thought a talking dog with a bouquet of wildflowers might be just the thing to brighten his mood. So he said to the prince, "There's someone outside I think you should see."

The prince turned from staring out the window, his hair impeccable, his suit perfect, and said, "Very well. But tell them to be brief."

The private secretary stepped back out and said to the dog, "Go right in." As the dog passed in front of him, he added, "Good luck," in a low voice.

Bowing grandly, the dog said, "A bouquet from the estate of the wealthy and powerful Jeffrey, as a very slight token of his very great esteem for you." He presented the flowers to the prince.

Well, the prince was charmed by the dog and spent some time talking with him of this and that. When it was time for the dog to go, the prince took a small pin from the lapel of his jacket, a copper pin shaped like a heart. "For the wealthy and powerful Jeffrey," he said. "With my compliments." The dog bowed once again and took his leave.

The private secretary came back in with a vase and began trimming and arranging the flowers. "How many men have you heard of," the prince mused, holding a sprig of jasmine to his nose, "who employ a talking dog as a messenger?"

"Counting the wealthy and powerful Jeffrey?" asked the private secretary. "One." And he was pleased that the prince's interest was aroused.

Meanwhile, the dog returned to the park where he'd left Jeffrey. On his way he stopped at a delicatessen. Rapping on the counter until he had the counterman's attention, the dog showed him the copper pin shaped like a heart. "I'm sure you recognize this," he said, with every show of confidence. "It's the prince's pin, presented just moments ago to my master, the wealthy and powerful Jeffrey, as a sign of the prince's very great esteem. Two of your finest sandwiches, and several small containers of the best your delicatessen offers, and I can promise you the prince himself will hear of your establishment."

The counterman raised his eyebrows. He recognized the pin—everyone knew of the prince's collection of heart-shaped pins—but he saw that it was the copper one. So he shrugged, made a tuna salad sandwich, wrapped it in white paper and pushed it across the counter to the dog. "Good appetite to the Jeffrey," he said, turning back to his work.

The dog took the tuna salad sandwich and returned to the park. Jeffrey was sitting just where the dog had left him, staring down at something that was neither here nor there. "Lunchtime," the dog announced in a cheerful voice, unwrapping the sandwich on the bench.

Jeffrey looked at the sandwich and shook his head. "I feel as if my heart has gone out of my chest," he said, and his voice was flat as a page of old newspaper. "I don't care if I never eat again."

"You have to eat something," the dog said sternly. "But as for your heart, here's a gift from the prince." He pinned the copper pin shaped like a heart to the front of Jeffrey's jacket. Well, the heart wasn't much, but it was something, and Jeffrey felt a little better. He took a bite of the sandwich, then went back to his staring. The dog sat beside him all afternoon, and that night Jeffrey slept on the bench with his head pillowed on the dog.

Next morning the dog was up before dawn. "Let's see if I can get us something better for our lunch today," he said, and off he went. He crept through the park until he came upon a pair of mockingbirds looking through the grass for worms. They were both so pleased with themselves for being up bright and early and so occupied in their hunt that the dog was able to catch them both. "Boys," he told them as he carefully pulled their flight feathers, "You've just run into a piece of good luck. You're going to live with the prince from now on. And all you have to do to ensure a totally luxurious existence is to sing for him." He taught them a variety of songs as he took them across the city, and after they'd gotten over their initial indignation, they proved to be quick studies.

The prince's private secretary had left word with the security guard and the receptionist that if a talking dog showed up, he was to be treated with all possible courtesy and shown in immediately. So it was that soon after his arrival, the dog found himself in the prince's office. He bowed. "From the wealthy and powerful Jeffrey," he said. "Something to brighten a dull hour, should you ever find yourself in one." He set the pair of mockingbirds down on the prince's desk. They hopped forward and broke into a medley of Broadway show tunes, coyly retiring after they'd finished behind the monitor of the prince's computer, only to be coaxed out for several encores.

The prince was delighted. He took off the pin he wore on his lapel, a silver pin shaped like a heart, and pressed it on the dog. "For the wealthy and powerful Jeffrey," he said. The dog bowed once more and left.

The private secretary came in with a cardboard box of mealworms and a pair of chopsticks. "Jeffrey, Jeffrey," the prince murmured, searching his memory. "Do I know a Jeffrey?"

"I'm sure you'd know it if you did," his private secretary said, giving one of the mockingbirds a mealworm with the chopsticks.

On his way to the park the dog stopped back in at the delicatessen. He showed the prince's pin to the counterman. "The wealthy and powerful Jeffrey continues to rise in the prince's favor," he said. "A smart businessman knows which side of his bread to put the butter on."

"Well, now, the silver heart-shaped pin," observed the counterman. "Let me see what I can do." He fixed two pastrami sandwiches, a pint of cole slaw, and some pickles, putting everything in a white bag. "Be sure to let the Jeffrey know I made that pastrami extra lean," the counterman called after the dog.

The dog carried the bag back to the park. Jeffrey sat on the bench, not quite at the same spot where the dog had left him, with his face in his hands and tears in his eyes. "I've brought lunch," the dog said gently, setting the food out beside Jeffrey.

"My heart's gone out of my chest," Jeffrey mourned, and his voice was like a river at the end of winter, still full of ice but beginning to flow again. "I don't want food."

"You have to eat," the dog chided him. "But as for your heart, here's a gift from the prince." He pinned the silver pin shaped like a heart over the copper pin, and because it was a little larger, the silver pin contained the copper one neatly. It was really quite a lovely heart, and looking down at it Jeffrey felt a bit better. He ate half of a sandwich, then went back to grieving and, occasionally, a brief walk. The dog stayed with him all afternoon, and that night, when Jeffrey lay down to sleep on the bench, his head was pillowed on the dog.

Next morning the dog searched quietly through the park until at last he spotted a squirrel spiraling down the trunk of a tree and venturing out onto the grass. In an instant the dog was on him. After a brief struggle, the dog brought his face very close to the squirrel's and emitted a long low growl that gave the squirrel an excellent view of his teeth. Then, keeping the toe of his loafer on the tip of the squirrel's tail, the dog sat up and said in a pleasant voice, "I need to ask an incredible favor of you."

"Anything," the squirrel said emphatically. "Anything at all."

"My very good friend the prince," the dog began, "has always longed for the company of a trained squirrel—"

"Say no more," the squirrel said, holding up one black paw. "There is no such thing as coincidence. I happen to have the most extensive repertoire of charming tricks of any rodent in the city. Why search any longer? Let's be on our way to your prince." And off they went.

In the prince's office, the squirrel proved as good as his word. He pulled quarters from the prince's ears, broke a watch to pieces inside a handkerchief only to pull it out again as good as new, and was very amusing with a deck of cards. As the finale to his act he chased his tail, pretending not to know it was his. The prince was mesmerized and applauded heartily when the squirrel finished. "Just delightful," he said. He took off the pin he wore on his jacket, a large gold pin shaped like a heart, and pressed it on the dog. "For the wealthy and powerful Jeffrey," he said. "Tell me, will he and I ever meet?"

"Of course, I can't make any promises," the dog shrugged. "But if you happened to be passing by the park tomorrow morning, it's entirely possible that you might run into the wealthy and powerful Jeffrey as he takes his prebreakfast jog." Then he bowed and left.

The prince's private secretary came in with a basket of acorns. "If that's his dog," the prince wondered aloud, "what do you suppose Jeffrey is like?"

"Absolutely fascinating, I'd imagine," the private secretary said, taking his watch back from the squirrel and giving him an acorn.

On his way back to the park, the dog stopped at the delicatessen. When the counterman saw the gold pin, he clapped his hands, and a boy came out from the back. "Assist me with the gentleman's order," the counterman cried. The two of them sliced prosciutto and Black Forest ham, wrapped smoked salmon and dusted off bottles of wine, brought out caviar and chocolate truffles. The counterman packed everything into a wicker basket with linen napkins and offered it to the dog, then held the door for him.

"Your generosity will be repaid," the dog promised, staggering out with the basket.

"For the Jeffrey, anything, anytime," the counterman said reverently, and then called after the dog, "And please remember, we deliver."

The bench was empty when the dog got to it, but he spread out the food and opened the wine. After a while Jeffrey returned. His hair was combed and he'd cleaned himself up. "Lunch?" the dog asked.

"My heart's gone from my chest," Jeffrey said impatiently. "Why do you keep bothering me about food?"

"You have to eat," the dog explained. "And as for your heart, look. A gift from the prince." He pinned the gold heart over the silver and copper ones, which fit into it so neatly that the three formed a single pin. It was beautiful, and looking at it made Jeffrey feel good. He sat on one end of the bench, the dog sat on the other, and between them they made a fine meal. Jeffrey spent the rest of the afternoon wandering through the park, smelling the flowers, or just sitting on the bench and watching the clouds pass by overhead. The dog kept him company. That night Jeffrey slept on the bench, and his head was pillowed on the dog.

Next morning the dog gently shook Jeffrey awake. "Take off your clothes and give them to me," the dog said.

"Why?" Jeffrey mumbled.

"We don't have a lot of time. Just do it," the dog urged him. Jeffrey did. The dog removed the gold pin shaped like a heart from Jeffrey's jacket and handed it back to him. "Whatever you do, don't lose this," he cautioned. Then he put Jeffrey's clothes in a trash can and hid Jeffrey in some bushes by the entrance to the park.

In a little while, the prince's car came by with the private secretary at the wheel and the prince in the backseat, anxiously looking out one window and then the other. The dog rushed out into the street. "Help!" he called. "Robbery! Police!"

The car stopped and the prince quickly rolled down the window. "Hello," he said. "What's the trouble?"

"Oh, thank heavens you're here," the dog cried. "The wealthy and powerful Jeffrey was just mugged as he took his prebreakfast jog. There must have been a dozen assailants. They took everything—his wallet, his silk warm-up suit, his aerodynamically perfect running shoes. Everything," and he paused for emphasis, "except the gold pin shaped like a heart. He fought for that like a tiger and finally drove off all thirty of them. But now, well, he finds himself in an embarrassing situation."

The prince's blood came to a quick boil when he heard that the wealthy and powerful Jeffrey had been assaulted, but settled to a gentle simmer at the idea that Jeffrey had fought such great odds to retain the heart-shaped pin. Fortunately, the prince never went anywhere without a complete change of clothing and footwear, and now he offered these to the dog for Jeffrey's use. The dog took them over to the bushes where Jeffrey waited, shivering, and helped him dress. "What's going to happen?" Jeffrey asked, lifting his chin so the dog could tie the knot in his tie.

"You're about to meet your admirer, the prince," the dog explained. He pinned the golden heart to the lapel of the jacket and stepped back. In the prince's suit Jeffrey looked like a prince. "Come," the dog said.

"I'm so sorry to meet you under these circumstances," the prince said, as the private secretary opened the door of the car for Jeffrey. "But so happy to finally meet you. May I give you a lift anywhere?"

"To the wealthy and powerful Jeffrey's estate," the dog said, getting in next to the private secretary. "I'll show you the way."

He directed the private secretary to the most fashionable neighborhood in the city while Jeffrey and the prince discovered how much each liked about the other. After a while the dog told the private secretary, "It's that house up on the right, the big one. I'll just run on ahead to make sure everything's in order."

"Good luck," the private secretary told him, and off the dog ran.

When he got to the house, a landscape architect and his assistants were engaged in moving a hill from one side of the grounds to the other. "Good morning," the dog said. "Tell me, please, whose house is this?"

"Why, this is the ogre's house," the landscape architect said. "And we work for him. Please don't interrupt us. We have to have this hill moved by lunchtime or things will be very unpleasant for us."

"You do fine work," the dog observed. "But I'm sorry to hear that you're doing this for the ogre. Because even as we speak, the prince is on his way at the head of his security forces to arrest the ogre and all his accomplices for crimes against the general population too numerous to mention. Look, there comes the prince's car now, and there are dozens more right behind it. I'm afraid you're in very serious trouble."

"We're not accomplices," the landscape architect protested. "We don't even get paid for our work. What will we do?"

"Perhaps there's a way out of this difficulty," the dog suggested. "If anyone asks, just say you work for the wealthy and powerful Jeffrey." The landscape architect promised he would and thanked the dog. The dog continued on up to the house.

A houseboy was sweeping off the front steps. "Good morning," said the dog. "Is this the ogre's house?"

"It certainly is," the houseboy said ruefully. "And if I were you, I'd keep walking until I came to a different one."

"Oh, I'm afraid I couldn't do that," the dog said. "The prince is on his way here at the head of all his security forces to arrest the ogre and all his accomplices. I've just come on ahead to make sure this was the right house. I hope you have a very good lawyer."

"I'm not his accomplice," the houseboy said indignantly. "I'm his houseboy, and I wouldn't be that if he hadn't said he'd eat me if I tried to leave. Now what am I supposed to do?"

"There's a very simple way out of this predicament," the dog said in a soothing voice. "If anyone asks, just say that you work for the wealthy and powerful Jeffrey. And please, keep sweeping. You're doing a splendid job. I'll just step inside to do a little preliminary investigating." And in he stepped.

The dog went through the house from top to bottom, making himself familiar with its rooms and all their contents. The last room of all was the ogre's study. When the dog quietly opened the door, there was the ogre himself, a little bit like a man, a great deal like a potato, only much, much larger, in a shabby black suit. Being an ogre, he had no heart of his own, and so he had taken to collecting hearts people lost to grief. He was busy with his collection now and had them spread out before him on his desk, so that he didn't hear the dog enter. Oh, he was having a splendid time with the hearts, sorting them, stacking them, holding them up to the light and grunting over them in a contented manner. The dog spotted Jeffrey's heart among the others. He cleared his throat.

"Who let the dog in here?" the ogre rumbled, throwing his arms around the entire heap of hearts and pulling them toward him. "Get out of here, mutt. Scat! Shoo!"

"Oh, don't mind me," the dog said in a friendly voice. "I'm just a neighbor stopping by to say hello. Say, that's quite a collection of hearts you have there."

"Don't you touch them!" the ogre growled.

"You needn't worry about me taking any of those," the dog sniffed, pretending to be offended. "They're all right, I suppose. Certainly not like some I've seen, though."

"You've seen better hearts than these?" the ogre asked, and in spite of himself his interest was piqued.

"I know a place where the hearts are much nicer than those," the dog assured him. "Bigger. Fuller. Why, in this place I know of, the people are so sad and grieving that the hearts just leap out of their chests. You catch them with butterfly nets."

"Really?" the ogre breathed. "Could we go there, do you think? By the way, would you like a bowl of water or anything?"

"No, thanks," the dog said. "I'd love to take you there, because I see that you're a real connoisseur. But I'm afraid you're just too large. You see, the entrance to this place is very, very small. You'd never fit through it."

"Is that all that's stopping us?" the ogre laughed. "Watch this." He took in a deep breath and blew it out, shrinking to half his former size.

"That's amazing," the dog said with deep admiration. "But no, you're still a bit too big."

"No problem," the ogre assured him. He exhaled again and shrank down by half. "Is this small enough?"

"Well," the dog said, coming around the desk to examine him. "You're getting there. I'm sorry to trouble you, but could you do that one more time?"

"I can do this all day long," the ogre boasted. He exhaled a third time and became truly tiny. "How's this?"

"Why, I believe that's perfect," the dog said, and he jumped on the ogre and chewed him up like an old bedroom slipper, spitting out the pieces because of the bitter taste. As soon as he had done so, all the hearts on the ogre's desk broke into song and rose into the air. The dog leapt up and caught Jeffrey's heart in the nick of time, just as all the hearts took a quick turn around the study and sailed away out the window.

Meanwhile, the prince's private secretary had lost sight of the dog. He pulled up in front of the house and said to the landscape architect, "Pardon me, but could you tell me who lives here?"

The landscape architect and all his assistants threw down their tools. "We work for the wealthy and powerful Jeffrey!" they cried. "We would never dream of working for anyone else."

"Well," the prince remarked to Jeffrey. "You certainly inspire loyalty in your employees." They drove up to the house.

The houseboy was sweeping the front steps. As soon as the private secretary opened the door of the car for Jeffrey and the prince, the houseboy dropped his broom and cried, "I work for the wealthy and powerful Jeffrey! I would never, under any circumstances, work for anyone else."

The dog came to the front door. "That's fine," he said to the house-boy. "Why don't you go prepare brunch for four? Come in everyone, and let me show you around."

He took Jeffrey to one side. "I've got something for you," he confided, showing Jeffrey the heart.

As soon as Jeffrey saw it, the heart lit up blindingly bright and flew back into his chest. "Oh," Jeffrey sighed. "Oh, that's so much better. I'd almost forgotten." The first thing he did was walk over to the prince. "Look," he said. "I'm not wealthy and powerful, I'm just Jeffrey. This house isn't mine, I've never even seen it before. My dog got it for me, though I have no idea how. So I think perhaps I should return your golden heart to you." He took the gold pin shaped like a heart off his jacket and held it out to the prince.

For the prince, this was the crowning touch. "I like you, Jeffrey," he said, smiling. "As far as wealth and power go, I've got enough of both, and they're not really that important to me. As for the house, I'd say if your dog got it for you, it's yours. And my heart—well, I wish you'd keep that, because you're the only man I've ever met whom I'd want to have it. So," he said, tucking his hand into the crook of Jeffrey's arm, "shall we go exploring your new house together?" And off they went, arm in arm.

The private secretary smiled at the dog. "Hmm," he said.

"Yes," the dog agreed. "Isn't it?" And they went into the parlor and had a long and pleasant chat about just what it is that makes the world go around.

THE FROG KING

THERE WAS ONCE a prince who had been blessed with a golden smile. He had been blessed with a number of other gifts as well—the face of an angel, abundant wavy hair, a body that responded well to exercise—but his smile was truly special. When he flashed it, locked doors swung open, problems solved themselves, and men were all attention and eagerness to please. This was important to the prince, whose name was Thomas, because he required a great deal of attention. It was as good as gold to him, and being a prince, he had a very expensive lifestyle. Actually, he lived in the guest house over someone else's garage, with two changes of clothes hanging in the closet and nothing in the little refrigerator but a jar of instant coffee. But the attention he got from men wherever he went was like a palace and a kingdom to him. He knew he could have whatever he wanted by flashing his golden smile, and so he lived without a care.

But the years passed, and as they did they helped themselves to Thomas's many gifts, like overnight guests who take the ashtrays and the towels and the silverware with them when they go. Men began to be less captivated by Thomas than they'd once been. For a long while Thomas didn't notice this, and when he did, for a long while he pretended not to.

"The Frog Prince, or Iron Heinrich," GB.

But a day came when Thomas looked around himself and realized he no longer lived in a kingdom but in a two-room guest house over somebody's garage. He wasn't sure why this had happened, but he knew that it had. "All I want is to stay a prince forever," he said to himself reasonably. "What's the problem?" Puzzled and unhappy, he went for a walk, trying to sort things out.

The lawn sloped down and away in a hillside behind the garage, and at the bottom he chanced upon a well he didn't recall having seen before. He peered over the rim. Far below, on the surface of the water, he saw his reflection. He gave a flash of his golden smile, and it looked as good to him as it always had. "Here's the problem," he said to himself. "My golden smile has fallen down this well. How will I fetch it out?"

Just then there was a disturbance in the water, and his reflection broke up and disappeared. Something leapt up out of the well, and Thomas scrambled aside. A frog landed on the grass next to him. Now, Thomas had never been much of a frog fancier, and this one was huge, as large as he was himself. Truth to tell, it looked very much like a bald, middle-aged man with an enormous belly and a face all bags and sags. "Ugh," Thomas cried, stepping away from it.

The frog didn't take offense. "Hello, Thomas," it said amiably. "Lose something?"

Well, Thomas wasn't inclined to let a frog start a conversation with him, and he was about to say something cutting. But it occurred to him that perhaps the creature could be useful. "Yes, actually, I have," he said, trying to keep the distaste out of his voice. "My golden smile has fallen down this well. Why don't you hop back down there and fetch it for me?"

The frog nodded its large head, considering this. At last it said, "What are you willing to give me?"

"I don't know," Thomas said, not wanting this to be a lengthy encounter. "What would you want?"

"What I want," the frog said, watching him steadily, "is to eat from your fork and drink from your cup with you. To lie with my head on your pillow and look into the mirror with you while you shave."

Thomas was outraged. "Never!" he cried, and stamped his foot. "Never, never, impossible!" The frog let him fuss, and when his anger had died down to a sulk, Thomas said, "Fine, OK. Go fetch my golden smile for me and I'll give you what you ask for."

"Give me what I ask for first," said the frog.

"That's not fair," Thomas protested.

"No," agreed the frog, not without sympathy. "But it's the way things are."

"Oh, all right," Thomas growled. "Come on, then." And he stalked off to his guest house over the garage.

"Walk more slowly, I can't keep up with you," the frog called after him. Thomas stopped, grinding his teeth. "I'm not as young as I used to be," it said when it caught up.

"Oh?" inquired Thomas coolly, looking at the repellent old creature from under lifted brows. "Were you young once?"

"Were you?" the frog countered.

"Excuse me," Thomas huffed. "I'm still young, thank you very much." The frog didn't say anything.

When they got upstairs, Thomas reached for the phone. "I'm ordering pizza," he said. "What do you like on it? Everything?"

"Pizza?" the frog laughed. "Oh, no—pizza gives me terrible indigestion; I'd be up all night with pizza. No, I need something with low fat, high fiber. Let's see. Order a piece of skinless broiled chicken and a salad. Light dressing."

"Right," Thomas sighed. "What about for dessert?"

"No, no dessert, thanks," said the frog, patting its generous belly. "I really don't need the calories." So Thomas phoned in their order. When the food came, they ate off the same fork and drank from the same cup, as agreed on. And though he was dying for something rich and sweet for dessert, Thomas had to admit that the light meal sat better on his stomach than his dinner usually did. "Delicious," the frog said, wiping his mouth with Thomas's napkin. "Well, now, let's read the paper for a while before we turn in."

"You turn in whenever you like," Thomas informed it. "I'm going out." Night, late night, had always been his favorite time. Late night was when everything was happening—adventures, excitements, unexpected encounters—and he wouldn't miss it for anything. But the frog had other ideas.

"You're not quite getting the point, Thomas," it said, as tactfully as possible. "We have to do everything together. Now, I can't stay up till all hours of the night, and that means you can't either, I'm afraid." And so it was that after they read the paper—the frog had an eye for the obituaries—they turned in, laying their heads down on the same pillow.

They woke up bright and early, and Thomas felt well rested and alert, though he usually slept in until noon and woke up groggier than when he'd gone to bed. The frog accompanied him into the tiny bathroom, and its face was right there in the mirror as he shaved. Oh, Thomas disliked the sight of the frog's face in his mirror—it was creased and pouchy and slack and not at all what a face should be. He rinsed off, dried off, and then said, "There. You've eaten from my fork and drunk from my cup with me, slept with your head on the same pillow and looked in the mirror with me while I shaved. I hope you enjoyed it. Now let's go to the well and get my golden smile out of it, because I've had all of your company I care for."

The frog cleared its throat—this took a while as it was very phlegmatic—and said, "Ah, Thomas. I'm afraid I'm not just an overnight guest."

"Excuse me?"

"What I mean is, I'm here to stay."

"Stay?" Thomas shrieked. "Never! Never, never, impossible!" And he threw himself down and beat the floor with his fists and feet, cried, and in general carried on until he was exhausted. But in the end there was nothing he could do. He sat up and looked at the frog, who was standing in the doorway, watching him patiently. "It isn't fair," he said hoarsely.

"No," the frog agreed in a gentle voice. "But it's the way things are."

"I *hate* you," Thomas told it, and he heaved a great shuddering sigh. "My life is over. I might as well die right now."

"Oh, well," the frog laughed, but then caught itself. "Look, it's a beautiful morning. Let's go out for a walk. You just need time to adjust to this."

"I'll never adjust to this," Thomas said miserably, but a walk didn't sound like such a bad idea.

They took several turns around the lawns out behind the guest house, and the frog kept a tactful silence. But every dead leaf Thomas came across reminded him that the delightful part his life was over. He was so wrapped up in his grief that he didn't notice that each turn around the grounds took them nearer and nearer to the forest that bordered the far edge of the property. Finally, with a light touch on his elbow, the frog guided Thomas in under the trees.

The two of them walked along on a path that was barely a path for some time, until they came to a men's clothing store, nestled among the trees. "Yes," said Thomas when he saw it. "Maybe a little shopping will make me feel better." In they went. He looked at neckties and sweaters, socks and blazers, but nothing really appealed to him. Then he saw some really lovely pants and decided to try on a pair. So he found them in his size. But the frog cleared its throat, and when Thomas glanced over irritably, it was shaking its head and indicating its bulky belly. "So?" Thomas demanded. "This is the size I always wear, a thirty-inch waist."

"Try these," the frog suggested, picking up the same pants in a thirty-two.

"Oh, come on," Thomas protested, but he took them into a dressing room and tried them on. He found that the thirty-twos didn't pinch him around the middle—he could actually breathe and the seat wasn't so confining. They were certainly more comfortable, but he was sad to no longer have the thirty-inch waist that had been his for so long. He paid for the pants and wore them out of the store.

"Those look very nice on you," the frog observed.

"Who asked you?" Thomas snapped.

They walked along, the path much easier to pick out now, and the frog tucked his arm through Thomas's. After a while they came to a gym, set back among the trees. "Great," said Thomas. "I'll feel better after a workout and a sauna. I always do." In they went.

Thomas undressed and walked into the weight room, the frog following. He began with some warm-up exercises, then stepped over to a rack of free-weights and selected a pair for his arm curls. The frog cleared its throat. "What?" Thomas growled.

"Maybe lighter weights this time?" it suggested, and put its hand to the small of its back. "We don't want to do any damage."

"These are the weights I always use for my arm curls," Thomas stated, and he began to do his curls. But he got tired faster than he usually did, the muscles in his arms started to tremble, and the curls didn't feel good at all. He brought the weights back over to the rack, but as he lifted them to set them in place he felt something snap like a wire in his lower back. "Gah," he cried, clenching his face in pain.

"The sauna," the frog said firmly. "It'll do you good." And so Thomas didn't finish his workout, he just had a long sauna. It made his back feel better, but he was sadder than ever to think that the big chest and strong arms, his for so long, would be his no more. They showered and left the gym.

The two of them walked along the path, the frog with his arm around Thomas's shoulders. It was very heavy. After a while they came to a bar, tucked among the trees. "I need a drink," Thomas said. In they went.

There was no one Thomas knew inside, no one who looked over at him in sudden interest, and the music was unfamiliar and too loud. He ordered his drink and sat at the far end of the bar, not even nursing the drink so much as keeping it company. A very attractive younger man came in, sat down at the other end of the bar, and ordered a beer. His eyes were like magnets, his attitude was very regal, and Thomas suddenly woke up out of his depression and wanted him as if he were the antidote to snakebite. But as he stood up to go and start a sparkling conversation with the younger man, Thomas caught sight of the frog's face in the mirror behind the bar. Even in the dim light it was not mistakable for anything but a frog's face. "What's the use," he groaned, setting down his drink and leaving. The frog, who'd finished its club soda, followed him.

Outside, it climbed onto his back, and a very heavy burden it was to carry, but that's what Thomas did. He'd never felt so miserable in his life. He trudged along and the path grew softer and stickier underfoot, until it ended ahead of him in a swamp. At the edge of the swamp grew a mangrove tree, and there, up on a branch of the tree directly overlooking the path, sat three frogs. Thomas was startled to see that they were even larger than the one he carried on his back. Not only that, but each of them wore a golden crown.

One frog sat with its back turned, while the other two faced forward, watching Thomas approach. As he drew near, one of them said, "So, how are things with you?"

He was about to say, "Miserable," when he realized it was addressing the frog on his back.

"Could be better, could be worse," replied Thomas's frog. "I'm putting on a few pounds, I've got a little lower-back pain."

"Tell *me* about putting on a few pounds," the frog with the golden crown commiserated, patting its fat belly. But it chuckled complacently.

"Tell *me* about lower-back pain," complained the second crowned frog, reaching around to massage the small of its back. But it chuckled as well and didn't seem particularly upset.

Then, as if it were the punch line to a joke they knew well and loved all the better for its being familiar, the two crowned frogs and Thomas's frog with them yelled, "Tell *me* about low scores at the bars!" and dissolved into fits of uncontrollable laughter. "Oh, oh, oh," they gasped. "What a world! What a world!" This only made them laugh all the harder. Thomas thought the two frogs would roll right off their branch, though for the life of him he couldn't see the joke. He waited until they had regained some of their composure before passing beneath them.

When he was on the other side of the tree, he turned around to look at the third crown-wearing frog. If he'd expected it to be jolly like the other two, he was disappointed. It sat there gazing peacefully out over the swamp. When it noticed him looking at it, the third frog frowned down on him. "Thomas," it said severely. "A frog without a crown is not a pretty thing."

Thomas knew it was referring to his own frog, but he didn't have any answer for it. He just stood there, terribly embarrassed.

When the third frog saw his discomfort, its expression softened. "There's quicksand in the swamp, you know," it remarked.

"What should I do?" Thomas asked humbly.

"Put that lazy frog down and make it carry you," said the crowned frog. Then it lifted its eyes from him and went back to regarding the swamp.

This made so much sense to Thomas that he couldn't understand how he hadn't thought of it himself. He set his frog down and asked, a little shyly, "Well. Would you carry me across the swamp?"

"Why, Thomas, I'd love to," answered the frog, its eyes sparkling. It lowered itself so he could climb on. "Step onto my head; you'll stay driest there." Thomas did. Then the frog stood up and set off into the swamp, balancing him on its head like a load of laundry.

And what a swamp it was! Not a harmless peat bog or picture-postcard estuary with cranes skimming the water, but the Swamp at the End of the World. It was all hanging mist and silence, blue scum and black water over bottomless oblivion. If Thomas had entered on his own, he would have sunk from sight at the third step—others had before him, how many no one knew. But the frog's natural buoyancy and big feet carried them both safely, and if anything, the wet refreshed and cheered the frog so that it whistled as it waded and sang as it swam. Finally they reached the other side, and Thomas was set back down on solid ground.

"I couldn't have gotten across that without your help," Thomas said, and he wasn't sure if he were speaking in gratitude or amazement. But either way, he held his hand out to the frog.

"No," the frog agreed. "You couldn't have." It took his hand and the two of them shook. "Well, shall we continue?"

There was no longer a path, but the two of them found their own way, chatting companionably of this and that. At last they came to the end of the forest and stepped out from under the trees. Now, that forest must have gone completely around the world, because in front of them was a busy street, and across the street stood the big house over whose garage Thomas lived. He'd never really noticed before how large the house was, more of a castle, really, with towers and pennants fluttering in the breeze. He and the frog waited for a break in traffic so they could cross.

At last a car stopped to let them walk. As they passed in front of it, Thomas saw that the driver was the younger man he'd seen in the bar. He nodded his thanks, and the younger man winked and gave him a smile, brief but blinding, and then roared off. It was just the flash of a smile, and almost impersonal, like the coin a rich man might toss to a poor man, thinking nothing of it. But Thomas recognized it at once.

"That was my golden smile," he said to the frog in amazement. "Did you see that? That kid had my golden smile."

"Yours once," the frog said, watching him. "His now. Someone else's later."

"Mine once, his now," Thomas repeated, and he nodded his head in agreement because he could see that this was so. "Well. I hope he enjoys it as much as I did."

"That's right," the frog laughed, nudging him. "Quite a world, isn't it?" And Thomas had to laugh as well, because it certainly was. They were walking up the drive of the white house now, but instead of continuing back to the garage and the tiny guest house, the frog took Thomas by the arm and led him up the lawn to the front door.

"What are you doing?" Thomas asked, because he'd never been to the main house before. "I'm not sure this is a good idea."

"Oh, I am," the frog replied. "As sure as sure."

Now, not only had Thomas never been inside the main house before but he had never met the owner. He'd come to live in the guest house over the garage when he was still a boy and just beginning to notice that men noticed him. At first he'd assumed the owner was a secret benefactor, who'd seen how special he was and who took pleasure in helping him, and this made perfect sense to Thomas; later on he forgot about the matter entirely. As the frog opened the front door, Thomas had a sudden idea. "You're the owner, aren't you?" he asked.

"The owner's picture is hanging inside," said the frog, and it stepped aside so Thomas could walk in. Thomas did.

It was a magnificent house, full of sunlight and deep shadow, with huge rooms opening into the distance off the entrance hall and vases of fresh flowers everywhere. A picture in an ornate frame hung on the far wall, a dust cloth draped over it. Thomas walked over and pulled the cloth away. He saw immediately that he'd been right, it *was* a picture of the frog. In the picture, though, the frog wore a golden crown, and this changed its appearance considerably. It looked wise, and peaceful, and ready to find the humor in anything, including itself. And there was something about its eyes, like the answer to a question Thomas had never known how to phrase. He leaned closer to see them better. As he did, the picture leaned closer to be better seen, and Thomas realized he was looking into a mirror. He blinked, and it wasn't a frog's face at all, just his own, a little older, but that was only to be expected. "Come and look at this," he called to the frog, laughing. "Come and see the owner of this fine big castle!" There was no answer.

Puzzled, he walked out to the front steps, but there was no frog to be seen anywhere on the lawn or the driveway or the street beyond; he called and called, but no frog answered. "He must have returned to his well," Thomas said to himself. "Just when I was getting used to him, too." And though he was sad that the frog had gone, there was a castle waiting for him to begin exploring its stairways and sunlit towers, its corridors and deep cellars. So he adjusted his golden crown and went back inside to do just that.

THE COMPANION

THERE WAS ONCE a young man named Jeremy, simple but sincere, who dreamed that he would have as his lover the most beautiful prince in the world. He went to his old father and said, "Last night I had a dream."

His father was reading the sports section. "That was just a dream," he told him, dismissing it. "Forget it."

That night Jeremy again dreamed of the prince who was to be his lover, slender and graceful and strong. He went to his father in the morning and said, "Last night I had the dream."

"So?" his father said from behind the business section. "I also had a dream last night. There was a kingdom, and you were ruling it. Does that seem likely? They're just dreams, son. They don't mean anything when you wake up."

That night, once again, Jeremy dreamed of his prince, who said to him, "I'm waiting. Where are you?" In the morning he went to his father and said, "I had the dream last night."

"So that's how it is with you?" said his father, setting aside the crossword puzzle. "In that case, you must go and search the world until you

"The Book of Tobit," A; "The Bald Man at the Funeral," AFT; thirteen versions from Europe and the Middle East, GDF; "A Dead Man Pays Back," GFT; "The Traveling Companion," HCA; "Fair Brow" and "Joseph Ciufolo, Tiller-Flutist," IF; "The Companion," NFT.

find your dream. Take your father's blessing with you wherever you go. You'll also need some money, and unfortunately I don't have much to give you. But take this little I've saved, and may it get you where you're going. And, son, try to remember: you're just a little bit simple, so be careful." Jeremy knew that his father was wrong about his being simple, but he kept that to himself. He embraced the old man and set out into the world.

Each morning he noted the point on the horizon where the sun rose. All day he walked until he reached that spot, and there he spent the night. On the morning of the fourth day, he happened to pass a cemetery. There was a disturbance at the gate. Mourners, pale, exhausted with grief, were trying to carry a coffin into the cemetery. But a man in a white lab coat had hold of one end of the coffin and kept pulling it back out. The mourners groaned and wailed and ground their teeth, but the man in the white lab coat was implacable.

"What's going on here?" Jeremy asked, pausing in his journey.

"My laboratory processed a panel of tests for this man," the man in the lab coat informed him, without relaxing his grip on the coffin. "Expensive tests. Complicated tests. Tests so complex it's impossible for a layperson to understand what's being tested, or why it costs so much. Well! The man died before we could get his results to him—these things happen sometimes. But now his friends and survivors refuse to pay the lab bill."

"We can't," the mourners cried, trying to pull the coffin into the cemetery. "There's no money left."

"Then sell the coffin!" roared the man in the lab coat. "Do whatever you want, do whatever you can, but until his bill is paid he's not going anywhere." And with that, he wrenched the coffin away from the mourners, dragged it out into the road and sat on it so it couldn't be budged.

Well, Jeremy's heart was touched by the mourners' distress. He took out his wallet and looked inside. "How much did he owe?" he asked.

"A lot," said the man in the lab coat. "How much have you got there?"

"Not very much," Jeremy admitted.

"Let's see," said the man, reaching into Jeremy's wallet. And by a strange twist of fate, it turned out that Jeremy had just enough for the man—"but only because I'm such a softy." The man in the lab coat left, thinking how lucky it was that he had met Jeremy, and the mourners carried the coffin into the cemetery, thinking how lucky it was that they had met Jeremy. Jeremy continued on his way, with nothing in his wallet but his social security card.

He walked along. After a while someone behind him called his name. He looked back over his shoulder, and there was a man running up the road. "Hello," said the man when he'd caught up. "You look like a young fellow who could use a servant."

"I don't see why," Jeremy said, reasonably enough. "I have nothing for a servant to do and nothing to pay him with for doing it."

"A companion, then," the man persisted. "There's no telling what odd jobs may need doing on the road ahead. As for wages, I'll be satisfied with half of whatever comes your way, good or bad." Well, it seemed like a bargain to Jeremy, so they shook hands, and it was done. The two of them walked on together.

After a while the road turned away from the place where the sun rose and ran toward a prosperous-looking village. Jeremy said, "Let's follow the road to that village. Some kind person is sure to take pity on us and give us food."

But his companion said, "No, you're headed in the right direction now. If the road doesn't go that way, it's time we left the road." And they did, setting out into the wild green country.

They walked until they came to a hill, directly in their path. The hill was too steep to climb, too wide to walk around, and covered with tiny white daisies nodding in the breeze. "How pretty," Jeremy said, because he dearly loved daisies. To his surprise, the companion, far from agree-ing, began tearing up great handfuls of flowers and throwing them over his shoulder. To his even greater surprise, when enough of the daisies had been torn away, a door was revealed in the hillside. The companion gave the door a knock, it opened, and in he went. Jeremy followed.

They made their way down a long low hallway until they found a room in the heart of the hill. A crooked little man stood before an enor-mous pot of soup, stirring and stirring it with a huge wooden spoon. He wasn't at all pleasant to look at, but when he noticed he had visitors, he gave them as sweet a smile as he could summon up. "Hello, boys," he said. "You're just in time for soup. It's my own recipe: I call it Every-thing-always-turns-out-for-the-best."

Well, it sounded good to Jeremy, but before he could say, "Yes, thank you," his companion said in a stern voice, "Have all your soup yourself." The crooked little man gave a cry of dismay and tried to jump aside, but before he could, a hand reached out of the soup, grabbed him by the scruff of the neck, and pulled him into the pot.

"Don't just stand there," he yelled, struggling with the hand. "Help me out of this!"

"You don't seem to have much of a taste for your own cooking," the companion observed, and it seemed to Jeremy he was in no hurry to offer assistance.

The hand gave the little man a good dunking. When he came up again, he cried, "Help me and I'll give you anything I possess, except one thing."

"And what's that?" asked the companion.

"My teaspoon of incredible depth," answered the little man.

"Well, then," replied the companion, "your teaspoon of incredible depth it will be, or we'll be on our way." The little man fretted and swore, but in the end there was nothing to do but tell them where the teaspoon was kept. The companion pocketed the teaspoon, left the little

man to get out of the pot as well as he could on his own, and led Jeremy
out by a side door back into the sunshine. Jeremy thought it was a bit
unfair to the little man.

The two of them walked on until they came to a second hill directly
in their path, too high to climb, too wide to go around. It was covered
with daffodils. "Oh, lovely," Jeremy sighed, because if there was anything he loved more than daisies, it was daffodils.

"They're all right, in their place," said his companion. This must not
have been their place, because he set to work tearing them up by the
bulbs as fast as he could. Soon he had uncovered a door that opened to
his knock. He went inside and Jeremy followed.

Down a long low hallway they went, and soon they stepped into a
room deep in the heart of the hill. A crooked little man stood before an
enormous pot of soup, stirring away at it with a huge wooden spoon. He
wasn't a little man who'd be winning any beauty contests, but when he
saw that he had company, he gave them a smile that surely he intended
to be welcoming. "You look hungry, boys," he said heartily. "What
about some nice hot soup? It's my own recipe: I call it Everyone-really-
wants-to-be-helpful-if-you-just-give-them-a-chance."

Well, it was an unlikely name for a soup, though Jeremy was willing to
give it a taste. But before he could say, "Yes, thank you," his companion
said in a voice like stones, "Have all your soup yourself." The crooked little man ground his teeth in rage and tried to hide under a stool, but a
hand rose out of the soup, knocked the stool aside, and pulled him into
the pot by his ear.

"Fine guests!" the little man shouted. "Get me out of this, and I'll give
you anything I own, except for one thing."

"And what's that one thing?" asked the companion.

"My salad fork of invisibility," the little man growled, trying to slap
the hand away. It slapped him back.

"Well, then, your salad fork of invisibility it will be," replied the companion, "or we'll be seeing you around some other time." The crooked little man called them sweet names and vile names, but at last he had to tell them which drawer he kept the salad fork in. The companion put the fork into his pocket with the teaspoon, took Jeremy by the arm, and led him out the back door into the sunlight.

They walked along. Now, Jeremy was curious why they hadn't let either of the crooked little men out of the soup after they'd gotten the unusual flatware from them. It seemed unfair, but he kept these doubts to himself, having noticed that his companion was a person to be reckoned with and who had his own way of doing things. By and by they came to a third hill, so tall the clouds had to walk over its top, so wide that it touched the horizon on each side. The hill was covered with rosebushes, and every bush was filled with the rosiest roses Jeremy had ever seen. "What do you think, Jeremy?" asked his companion. "Nice roses?"

"They're all right, I guess," answered Jeremy, not quite as enthusiastically as he once might have. He grasped one of the bushes and tried to pull it up. But the roots went too deep, and all he managed to do was get his hands stuck with thorns. His companion moved him aside, tore several bushes out of the hillside, and there was a door that opened to his knock. In they went, down a long low hall to a room deep in the heart of the hill.

Here as well a crooked little man stood before an enormous pot of soup, and he was by far the crookedest of the little men they'd come upon yet, like a jigsaw puzzle someone hadn't the patience to put together the right way. But oddly arranged or not, he was still quite able to stir his soup with a huge wooden spoon. When he saw that he had guests, he gave them each a smile like first love and cried, "Just in time, you lucky boys! Soup's ready, and it's my own, my very own recipe: I call it Every-ending-is-a-happy-one-so-why-not-relax-and-enjoy-yourself."

Well, even Jeremy knew that wasn't a fit soup to eat, no matter how hungry you were. Before his companion could speak, Jeremy cried, "Have all your soup yourself!" The crooked little man threw him a look like a chainsaw and tried to run, but before he could take two steps a hand shot out of the soup, grabbed him by the seat of his pants, and hauled him into the pot.

"Ugh, needs salt," snarled the little man, beating at the hand with his huge wooden spoon. The hand wrested the spoon from him and gave him a good whack. "Get me out of this and I'll give you anything I have."

"Except?" prodded Jeremy.

"Except my steak knife of unfailing sharpness," said the little man in a reasonable tone of voice. "You couldn't expect me to let you have that."

"Could we?" Jeremy asked his companion.

"We certainly could," his companion replied. "Your steak knife it will be, or it's been nice seeing you." Well, the little man suggested several things they could do to themselves with common household objects, but finally he had to tell them which steak knife on the rack was the one of unfailing sharpness. The companion took it, out the back door they went and on their way in the sunlight.

They walked along, and Jeremy reflected that if the way to the prince of his dreams was stranger than he'd expected, he had certainly found someone every bit as strange to travel it with. Suddenly his companion said, "Run, Jeremy," and began to do so himself.

"All right," Jeremy said. "But why?" His companion just pointed behind them and kept on running. When Jeremy looked back, whom did he see but the three crooked little men. Only now they weren't little men at all, they were enormous and not in very good moods. Though they were still as crooked as could be, their running skills were remarkably unhampered, and each covered a mile at a step. Well, Jeremy and his companion ran for all they were worth, but soon their pursuers were almost upon them. Just when it seemed that the journey would have an unpleasant end, the companion reached into his pocket, took out the teaspoon of unbelievable depth, and threw it back over his shoulder.

The first enormous crooked man didn't even see the teaspoon and fell right in. The second enormous crooked man saw it and stopped in the nick of time. But the last enormous crooked man was so terribly crooked that he ran looking behind himself. He slammed into the second, and the two of them tumbled into the bowl of the teaspoon. Jeremy waited a moment, but when nothing else happened, he walked back to the teaspoon and looked into it. Not only was it empty, but the bowl was so deep the sunlight couldn't reach the bottom of it. He picked the spoon up and brought it back to his companion, who put it away again. The two of them walked on.

After a long while the wild green country gave place to a land of bleakness, barrenness, and the sharp frosts of winter. In the middle of the land stood an enormous castle. The flags flying from it were black, and a fence of one thousand iron spikes surrounded it. On every spike but one a man's head was impaled. "This is the castle of the King Behind the Sunrise," Jeremy's companion told him.

Jeremy was about to suggest they put the castle behind them as soon as possible when he happened to look up. There, at the highest window of the tallest tower, staring out impassively at the wintery landscape, was the prince of his dreams. "We're here!" Jeremy cried to his companion. "Let's go inside." Which is what they did, and in a very short time they were standing in the court of the king.

The king's courtiers wore silver and gold, and the king himself wore gold and diamonds. In spite of the splendor that surrounded him, the king's face was full of lines, and all the lines pointed down. "So," he said, and Jeremy had never realized how discouraging the word could sound. "I suppose you've come to try your hand at winning the prince. No doubt you noticed the nine hundred and ninety-nine heads as you came in. Those are the suitors who couldn't perform the three tasks my son set them. If you can, you win William, as well as half of my kingdom. If you can't, well, there's still an empty spike." He sighed wearily and shook his head. "He used to take pleasure in such simple things. Now all he wants to do is have people's heads cut off. Look," he said, appealing to Jeremy in a reasonable tone of voice. "You seem like a very nice young fellow. Stay, have some supper, we'll give you a nice room for the night. Tomorrow you can be on your way again. Go kill some dragons, go break some magic spells, go anywhere you like. What do you say?"

Grateful to finally have a chance to speak, Jeremy shook his head vehemently and said, "Oh, no. I'll stay and try my hand at winning the prince—I dreamed of him three nights in a row."

"I hope you've got three more nights ahead of you to dream in, young fellow. Don't say I didn't warn you," the king sighed. Just then the door of the throne room opened. "My son, Prince William," announced the king with great irony, and William entered.

He was even more beautiful than in Jeremy's dream, slender and graceful and strong. But he was cold—colder than sweaters could warm, colder than joy could touch, colder than words could reach. This wasn't what Jeremy had been expecting at all, and he approached William hesitantly. "My name's Jeremy," he said. "How do you do?"

"I'm William," William replied, and even his breath was icy. "I'm going to die. And you are, too, if you try to win me." Which pretty much put a lid on any further small talk. Fortunately, dinner was announced, and the entire court moved into the banquet hall.

Jeremy found himself seated next to William at the table. William allowed no food to be put on his own plate but contented himself with occasional sips of stagnant water. While everyone else ate, he read the *Tibetan Book of the Dead*, pausing every once in a while to look disdainfully around him at the members of the court, who all had hearty appetites.

When the table was cleared, William turned to Jeremy. "Your first task," he said in an empty voice, "is to keep something for me tonight and give it back when I ask for it tomorrow." He handed Jeremy a golden cock ring. Jeremy, who thought he'd be told to bring the moon on a Ritz cracker or something equally challenging, was elated. He put the cock ring in his pocket. Then William's manner changed completely. He became convivial and flirtatious, drew Jeremy out and made him laugh, and filled his glass again and again until Jeremy's head spun with all the wine and attention.

Meanwhile, the companion excused himself early from the table and went down to the kennel. There were a great many dogs there, greyhounds and mastiffs and magnificent hunting poodles, all of them in splendid condition but all of them contentedly asleep. At last he came to a sheltie, wide awake, with long don't-touch-me-I'm-blond fur and a bitter expression around its muzzle. "What time does the prince take you for your walk tonight?" asked the companion.

"What sort of fool expects a dog to answer questions?" the sheltie sneered, and then too late realized it had given itself away. "Eleven-thirty," it grumbled. Satisfied, the companion went up to his room.

When the evening came to a close, Jeremy bid William good night and went up to his own room. He undressed and, for safekeeping, put on the golden cock ring, then lay down and fell heavily to sleep.

William went up to his tower but didn't undress. Instead, he called softly, and a cat the color of something difficult to see detached itself from the shadows. He sent it creeping down to Jeremy's room. The cat crouched on Jeremy's chest, watching him, and every time he took a breath the cat stole half of it, with the result that Jeremy began having terrible dreams. After a while the cock ring slipped off, and the cat carried it in its mouth back to William.

At exactly eleven-thirty, William went down to the kennel to take his sheltie out for a walk. But the companion, with the salad fork of invisibility pushed into his hair like a comb, was waiting unseen at the door of the kennel.

William leashed the sheltie and said, "Come on, boy. You know the way," and the dog took off like a shot, with William running behind. When it reached the door of the kennel, the dog gave a sudden leap into the air. As William's feet left the ground, the companion seized hold of the lace of one of his Reeboks, and off into the night sky they went.

The dog flew over the frozen fields, over a forest, over mountains, over the sea, until it approached a great rock far far out in the water, and there it came down. It lifted its leg against the face of the rock and urinated, and where the urine hit, a door opened. William went inside, the companion walking quietly behind him. Within the rock was a furnished single apartment, within the apartment lived a ghoul, and the ghoul was waiting for William.

Now, William was very studious and had learned to do a number of amazing things—such as teach a dog how to talk and fly. But the day he learned he was fated to die, something long and cold coiled in his stomach, making a home for itself, and all his reading and studying seemed pointless. He decided to go in search of Death to see if somehow he could strike a bargain with that powerful figure. He hadn't found him. Instead, he'd met the ghoul, who claimed to be Death's brother, though in fact he was only a distant cousin many times removed, whose only contact with Death was the card the ghoul sent him each year at Christmas—a card that was never reciprocated. But the ghoul had taken one look at William, wanted him, and lied through his crooked teeth. "Oh, sure, me and him are just like this," he'd said, holding up his crossed fingers by way of illustration. "He never makes a move without asking my advice. Listen, if I say the word, your life will be spared forever. Maybe we can work something out." So William had become lovers with the ghoul, visiting him each night after everyone else was asleep. The ghoul insisted that William have no other lovers, always pressuring the prince to move in with him. William had at first resisted, but under the ghoul's influence life had lost all its joy, and gradually the idea of coming there to stay had begun to seem, if not more attractive, then not as repulsive as it once had. The ghoul's only fear was that William might somehow discover that he himself actually possessed more knowledge and power than the ghoul ever would.

"Here," William said, handing the golden cock ring to the ghoul. "I've got another suitor, and tomorrow his head will go on the one-thousandth spike for want of this."

"Good," the ghoul laughed, and he tossed the cock ring into the drawer of a dresser that was filled with such rings. But the companion caught it and put it away in his pocket. "Who's the only one in the world you love?" the ghoul whispered eagerly.

"You," William sighed, moving into the ghoul's arms. They lay down together on a couch carved of marble, and William remained in the ghoul's embrace, silent and staring straight ahead at nothing, all night long.

Just before dawn, William got up, kissed the ghoul good-bye, and left his apartment. He leashed his sheltie and cried, "Let's go, boy! You know the way back." The dog leapt into the air, the companion caught hold of the lace of William's Reebok, and away they went, over the sea, over the mountains, over the forest, over the frozen meadows, and down again at the door to the kennel. William climbed up to the tower to change his clothes.

The companion went to Jeremy's room and shook him awake. "Do you still have what the prince gave you last night?" he asked.

"Right here," Jeremy mumbled, but when he felt for it, the cock ring wasn't right there at all. He threw back the covers and searched the bed, then turned to his companion and said, "I think I'm in trouble. What should I do?"

The companion handed the cock ring to him. "Give it to the prince when he asks for it," he said.

William browsed through an anthology of epitaphs during breakfast. When everyone else had finished eating, he marked his place and said to Jeremy, "I suppose you've still got what I gave you. I'll have it back now."

"Certainly," Jeremy replied, and threw the golden cock ring down into the empty plate in front of William.

William's eyes narrowed to chips of ice when he saw it, but the king, who had been prepared to send for the executioner, was overjoyed. "He's performed the first task," he cried. "Today's a holiday!" And so it was, with feasting and entertainments and Judy Garland impersonations. But William excused himself from the table and wasn't seen again until dinner.

After dessert was served, William unbuttoned his shirt and removed a tiny gold ring from his left nipple. "Take this and keep it for me until I ask for it again," he told Jeremy. Jeremy received the ring, and though he had resolved not to drink so much, in order to be more alert, William once again became charming and engaging and filled his glass over and over. Jeremy, intoxicated with William, drank, with the result that when he went up to bed, after putting the gold ring through his own nipple for safekeeping, he fell into sleep as if his bed were deep water.

The companion had slipped away from the table during dinner and gone down to the kennel. "What time does the prince take you for your walk tonight?" he asked the sheltie, but the dog merely gave him a haughty look and refused to speak. The companion took out some meat he'd saved from his plate. "Hungry, boy?" he asked, and of course the dog was. "Can you roll over, boy?" he asked, and the dog did. The companion threw him a piece of meat. "Sit up and beg, boy," he said, and the dog did. The companion threw him another piece of meat. He held the biggest piece of meat over the dog's head. "Now, speak, boy," he commanded. "Speak!"

"Quarter to twelve!" the dog barked ecstatically, and then, too late, realized it had been tricked.

Meanwhile, William had sent his cat the color of a shadow in the shade to get the gold ring back from Jeremy. The cat crept into Jeremy's room and pulled the covers down from his chest. It slipped the tip of its tail through the ring, and then it pushed its tail through a little further, and a little further still, until at last the ring sprang open. The cat brought the ring in its mouth to William, who put it in his pocket and went down to the kennel.

The companion was there already, the salad fork of invisibility in his hair. William leashed his sheltie, said, "Let's go, boy. You know the way," and off through the air they went, with the companion slipping his little finger through a belt loop of William's pants. They flew over the fields, over the forest, over the mountains, and far out over the sea to the rock where the ghoul lived. The dog lifted its leg, the door opened, and William went in with the companion right behind him.

The ghoul was waiting for him. "I thought you said you were powerful," William spat.

"I am powerful," the ghoul blustered, hating it when William was full of energy. "I'm very powerful. I am extremely powerful."

"But this morning my suitor gave me back the golden cock ring," William raged at him. "I'm one-third his. Now take this and put it where no one will ever find it."

The ghoul took the tiny gold ring from him. "Hey, come on, you're getting yourself all worked up. You know that's not good for you," he soothed. "I've got just the place for this." He stared at the floor and intoned in a drab monotonous voice,

> "Life is short and death is long.
> Life is weak, but death's real strong.
> Laugh, or sing, or dance around—
> you'll lie quiet in the ground."

The floorboards shivered, then slid apart to reveal an open grave. The ghoul dropped the gold ring into it. But as the ring left his hand, the companion caught it in his own and put it away in his pocket.

William heaved a sigh of relief and surrendered himself to the ghoul's embrace. The ghoul brought him over to the marble couch and murmured to him all night long of cemeteries, and funeral arrangements, and what happens to the light when you flick off the light switch.

Dawn approached and William rose from the ghoul's couch and kissed him good-bye. Outside, he leashed his dog, cried, "Come on, boy! You know the way back." The companion hooked his finger through William's belt loop, and back they all went, over the sea, over the mountains, over the forest, over the fields, and down again at the door to the kennel. The companion went to Jeremy's room and shook him awake.

"Do you still have what the prince asked you to keep for him?" he asked.

"Right here," Jeremy said, putting his hand over his heart and then taking it away, empty. "I don't believe this."

"Really?" asked his companion. "I do. You might try bearing in mind that you're a little bit simple."

"No, I'm not," Jeremy protested, but under his companion's stern gaze he had to lower his head in agreement. "Well, maybe a little bit. What should I do?"

"Give this to the prince when he asks for it," his companion said, handing the gold ring to Jeremy.

At the breakfast table everyone was tense, waiting to see if Jeremy had performed the second task. William came in carrying a prospectus from a large chain of cemeteries and sat next to him. "I'll have back what I gave you last night," he said. "Unless you've misplaced it, of course." And he permitted himself a small smile.

"Not at all," Jeremy replied, tossing the gold ring into William's plate.

"Yes!" the king cried. "Two down, one to go. Nobody works today." Jugglers ran in and began tossing dishes up into the air, the pastry chefs brought out cakes with so many layers that the tops couldn't be seen, and clowns made animals out of balloons. But William fled up to his tower and spent the day sobbing and baffled.

That night he took the gold earring from his ear and presented it to Jeremy. "Keep this for me," he said. Then he looked deep and deep into Jeremy's eyes until he reached his heart, where he made promises of impossible happiness. Jeremy, remembering that he was a little bit simple, did his best not to believe everything he saw in William's eyes. And while this was difficult, he might actually have succeeded if William hadn't dropped a tiny pill into Jeremy's glass and given it to him to drink. When Jeremy went up to his room that night, he just had time to put the earring in his own ear for safekeeping before sleep came on him like a mountain rolling over.

The companion slipped away to the kennel. When the sheltie saw him, it growled deep in its throat and began snapping. "I was thinking about you during dinner," the companion said. "You know, with all the unloved and homeless puppies there are in the kingdom, the responsible thing to do would be to have you neutered."

"Nice man," the dog whined. "Tonight I go for my walk at midnight, nice man."

Meanwhile, William sent his cat the color of a glass of water in a dark room to Jeremy. It crept up next to Jeremy's head, put its mouth against his ear, and purred until the earring fell onto the pillow. Then it picked the earring up in its mouth and brought it to William. William went down to the kennel, leashed his dog, and said, "Let's go, boy. You know the way." The companion, the salad fork of invisibility stuck in his hair, caught hold of a hair on William's head, and away through the night sky they flew. As they did, the companion whispered to William, "You're wasting your life, stupid!"

"Why am I suddenly full of self-doubt about what I'm doing?" William wondered aloud as they flew over the fields, over the forest, over the mountains, and out over the sea to the ghoul's rock. He went in, the companion close behind him, and as soon as he saw the ghoul, William cried, "You said you were strong! You said you were powerful! How can you keep me safe when you can't even hold onto a ring? He returned it to me this morning. Don't let him win me, it hurts too much." He began to weep.

When he saw William weak, the ghoul puffed out his sunken chest as much as he could. "Nothing can take you away from me," he roared. "Nothing can touch you when you're in my arms—not the night air, not the morning dew, not the light of day—"

"And not Death," William reminded him tearfully.

"Uh, right. Him, either," agreed the ghoul, deflating, and he changed the subject. "What's the third thing this guy's supposed to keep for you?"

"This," said William, holding out the gold earring.

"No problem," the ghoul growled, fastening the earring into his own ear. "He'll have to cut my head off to get it, and I'd like to see him try." Actually, the last thing in the world the ghoul wanted to see was someone trying to cut off his head—it had always been a particular fear of his.

To assuage this fear, he wore a special studded collar that had been guaranteed by the man who'd sold it to him to be absolutely impervious to everything, except the steak knife of unfailing sharpness. And since *that* was the property of an old acquaintance with whom the ghoul went out of his way to maintain good relations, he felt safe. Not totally safe, but as safe as a person could feel in a horrible, unpredictable world like this. "Now come here," he ordered. William closed his eyes and went to him gratefully, and the ghoul bore him over to the marble couch, where they lay down together. He put his cold dry mouth to William's ear, and all night long he whispered the story of nothing, which hasn't much of a beginning, even less of a middle, and no ending at all.

Dawn came, and William kissed the ghoul good-bye and went outside. The ghoul, being a little stiff, put his hands to the small of his back and stretched. As he did, the companion came up behind him, whipped out the steak knife of unfailing sharpness, and swept the ghoul's head off with a single blow. Then he put the head inside his jacket, ran out of the apartment, and caught hold of one of William's hairs just as the dog leapt up into the air.

As they flew, the companion whispered to William, "Stupid! Wimp! Everything that lives has to die," and struck him again and again.

"When this thousandth suitor's head is on a spike," William promised himself, "I'll move in with the ghoul and be safe forever." They flew over the sea, over the mountains, over the forest, over the frozen fields, and came down at the door of the kennel.

The companion ran up to Jeremy's room and tried to shake him awake, and when that failed he threw a basin of cold water on him. "Do you still have what the prince asked you to keep for him?" he asked.

"It's right here," Jeremy muttered thickly, putting his hand to the side of his head. But it wasn't, and he sat up with a groan. "No, not again! I'm more than just a little simple; I should be interviewing for a village idiot's position."

"Well, actually, Jeremy, you're in love," said his companion dryly. "And you were medicated. It's difficult to stay alert under those conditions." He pulled the ghoul's head out from under his jacket, the golden earring gleaming in the ghoul's ear. "Here. Give this to the prince when he asks for it," he said.

Jeremy woke up completely. "What *is* that?" he cried.

"This is what you're competing with for the prince's affections," his companion said. "Don't be such a baby. Put it in a pillowcase and give it to the prince when he asks you for his earring." So Jeremy dressed, put the head in a pillowcase, and took it down to breakfast.

Everyone at the breakfast table was silent and waiting for him as he took his seat. Then William came in and sat down, and if there was triumph in his face there was sorrow as well. "Of course you still have what I gave you last night," he said. "Give it back to me now—unless you've misplaced it?"

"No, I have it here," Jeremy said, and with that he pulled the ghoul's head out of the pillowcase and thumped it down in William's plate. The king and all his courtiers and servants gasped.

"I'm lost," William whispered. His eyes rolled up white in his head, and he slid off his chair onto the floor.

The king was the first to recover himself. "Jeremy has won the prince and half of the kingdom," he announced in a shaky voice. "But, um, could you perhaps get rid of that thing before we begin the celebration?"

The companion removed the earring from the ghoul's ear and handed it to Jeremy. Then he took out the teaspoon of unbelievable depth, dropped the ghoul's head into the bowl, and put the teaspoon away again. There was a great sigh of relief from everyone present. Then the air was full of confetti, horns were being blown, and everyone was dancing—courtiers with servants, soldiers with nobles, while the king climbed onto the table and did a jig among the dishes. William was re-vived with cold water and smelling salts, but all he did was stare ahead of him at nothing and shake his head.

"It's time for me to go," the companion said to Jeremy amid all the noise. "We need to talk about my wages. Bring William into the next room." So Jeremy gently took William by the arm and followed his companion into the next room. His companion closed the door. "If you remember, Jeremy, we agreed that half of everything that came your way would be mine. Now, I can't take half of your half of the kingdom with me. But I can take half of William." And he brought out the steak knife of unfailing sharpness.

"Now wait a minute," Jeremy said, alarmed.

"Did you give me your hand on the bargain or didn't you?" his companion demanded.

"Yes, I did," Jeremy admitted miserably.

"Good," said his companion. He gathered the front of William's shirt in his fist and said in a voice like iron on stone, "Now hold still. I want to make sure I cut you in two equal pieces." And he raised the steak knife over his head.

"No!" William cried out, and cried out with such force that he vomited up a truly enormous black serpent. With a flash of his knife, the companion cut the serpent in two equal pieces, head and tail, and ate them both.

"There," he said, wiping his mouth on the back of his hand. "That'll be my share. We had to get *that* out of you, or you would have just gone back out and found yourself another ghoul. Which would have been bad news for Jeremy."

As soon as he'd vomited up the serpent, a flush of warmth rose into William's face. "I can't believe it's finally over," he laughed, tears streaming from his eyes. "When I learned I was going to die, the whole world went cold. I thought the ghoul could protect me, but all he did was make me not care about anything. Thank heavens, everything's all right now—I'm not going to die." And he smiled radiantly, waiting for them to confirm this for him.

Before Jeremy could, his companion frowned and said, "Not going to die? I thought Jeremy was the simple one. Of course you're going to die, William." William's face began to go pale again. The companion leaned forward, and tapping William's chest with his forefinger for emphasis, he said sternly, "You, your father, Jeremy—everyone you know and everyone you don't know. Depend on it: all of you will die."

Well, Jeremy had agreed to give his companion half of everything that came his way, but he'd said nothing about letting him bully the man of his dreams. "What do you mean, 'all of you'?" he demanded, stepping forward and putting his arm around William's shoulders. "What about you? What makes you so special?"

Then his companion laughed for the first time since Jeremy had met him, a laugh deep in the belly that went on and on until Jeremy began to get quite annoyed. "Why, Jeremy," he gasped, when he could speak

again. "I'm already dead. I'm the man whose lab bill you paid so he could
be buried. And now that I've repaid you for your kindness, I'll be on
my way."

"But where are you going?" William broke in. "What happens—"

"No," said the companion, cutting him off.

"But—"

"*No*," repeated the companion, and the word dropped from his
mouth like a mountain there was no getting around. "*Now*. Now is the
time for you to decide whether you'll take a lover or live alone, whether
you'll stay inside reading a book or if you'll go outside in the weather for
a walk, whether you prefer up or find down more to your liking. Now
you make choices, and what comes later, you'll do later." But William
looked so forlorn and Jeremy so puzzled that the companion relented,
just a little. "All right," he conceded. "I'll show you as much as I can."

He stepped up to the nearest wall and touched it with the tip of his
finger. Immediately the wall slid aside like a curtain, opening onto a long
view of green meadows and, far in the distance, the sea, like a placid band
of blue with the clear blue sky above it—though by rights, all that
should have come into sight was the inside of the linen closet next door.
A walkway of white marble stretched clear to the far sea, and the delicate
white pillars lining it supported delicate white arches. Through the arch
at the end of the walkway could be seen a bit of blue horizon and the
cloudless sky, and it was very lovely. But just where the walkway began,
almost at their feet, a large piece was broken away, and Jeremy and
William saw that a stone tunnel, empty of everything except darkness,
ran just under the white walkway.

"Well, boys," said the companion. "What do you think of the way
there?"

"It's beautiful," breathed Jeremy, looking at the white path.

"It's horrible," whimpered William, looking into the lightless tunnel.

"That's right," confirmed the companion. "Now, watch carefully, boys, because I'm only going to do this once." Without saying another word, he stepped out of the room, putting his foot down on the white path. As he did, he put his foot into the dark tunnel. Now, it's not that he became two companions, nor that the white path sank down into the tunnel or that the floor of the tunnel rose up to the level of the path. Jeremy and William took a step forward themselves, trying to see better what exactly was happening. But at that moment, the wall slid back in place, and they could no longer see either the way or its traveler.

When it became apparent that the companion wouldn't be coming back, William turned to Jeremy. "Well," he said tentatively. "What should we do now?"

"Get you something to eat and drink," Jeremy said firmly. "You must be starving." William was, but they wound up in each other's arms instead, laughing, and crying, and singing, and all those things lovers delight in.

So Jeremy won William, as well as half of the kingdom. The old king was so pleased with the way things turned out that he gave the other half of his kingdom to William. The land flourished under their rule, and if neither William nor Jeremy lived forever, they lived intensely, delighting in each moment as if it were a gift waiting to be unwrapped. Which, of course, it is.

The Man Who Came
Back from the Dead

THERE WERE TWO friends. Perhaps they were lovers; perhaps they were brothers. The important thing is that they loved each other and thought they had their whole lives ahead of them—seven, eight, nine hundred years. There was no hurry; they had time to grow bored with each other, time to fight about nothing much, time to forget because there was time to remember again.

One of them got sick. He wasn't supposed to; he did anyway. He died. One day he was sitting there, same as always; next day he was in his coffin. If he was a friend, all the friends came to the funeral; if he was a lover, all the lovers came; if he was a brother, the whole family was there. The one who was left sat beside the coffin after everyone went home again. What did he do? He cried.

The one who died went to the other world. When he got there, they were playing cards. "Pull up a chair," they said, "we'll deal you a hand." He did. After a while, they said to him, "You know, you've been forgotten already back where you came from. No one's crying about you anymore."

"You're wrong," he said. "Everyone's still crying."

"Jorška Who Came Back from the Dead," GFT.

"No, you've been forgotten," they told him.

He got so curious that he went back to find out. He sat up in the coffin. The one who hadn't died was still there, crying. He was scared when the one who died sat up. He didn't know what to do; he became confused. "You're dead," he told him.

"I came back," said the other. "You're still crying. That's good. But what about all the others? Are they still crying, too?"

"Let's see," said the first. He called to all the others, "He's come back!" Everyone came running to see. Some were still crying, some weren't.

"I've come back," said the one who'd died. "If you'd all still been crying, I could have stayed with you for many years. As it is, I can only stay for six weeks." Everyone, the friends, the lovers, the whole family, decided to feast him for the six weeks he'd be with them.

This feast is still going on. Now is the time to bring him his favorite dish. Now is the time to buy him a new shirt. And if you're ever going to tell him how good his hair looks when he steps out of the shower, now is the time.

This is a true story.

This work was blessed with many fairy godfathers;
to these gentlemen, gratitude:

Benjamin Barker

Kevin Bentley

Robert Drake

Eric Gordon

Daniel Harris

Robert Hopcke

Steve Johnson

Rondo Mieczkowski

William Moritz

Kieran Prather

Andrew Printer

Rick Sandford

Stuart Timmons

Andrzej Wilczak

Brian Williams